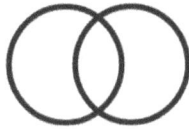

hidden.
Self-Published by Marcos D. Torres

ISBN: 978-0-6450366-7-1

For permissions or information contact:
pastormarcos@thestorychurchproject.com

Cover and graphics designed on Canva

www.thestorychurchproject.com

To all those people who have ever wondered
if there is more to "church."

To my family, the R3 Network, and the Western Australia Conference, thank you for all your support.

CONTENTS

FOREWORD

Twelve years ago, I began pastoring my present church—and I'll never forget one thing my head elder warned me about when I arrived.

"If you preach the gospel here," he explained, "you're going to upset people."

This wasn't a threat on his part. He loved the gospel and longed to have it proclaimed. He was just letting me know what to expect if I planned to talk about God's boundless love and radical grace.

So, do you know what I did?

Week after week after week I preached my heart out, proclaiming the beautiful gospel.

And do you know what happened?

Nothing.

Nothing happened.

No one got upset.

No one left the church because I was preaching a gospel of "easy grace."

In fact, it felt like, to some degree, people just became more comatose with each passing week.

A few years later, I preached a series of sermons—consisting of seven or eight talks—about sex that at times got a little explicit (in retrospect, I don't think I should have preached the series but—that's a story for another day).

And do you know what happened?

Nothing.

Nothing happened.

No one got upset.

No one left the church because I was preaching about a controversial topic.

But then something strange happened. I finally got people upset—to the point that some started leaving the church.

And what was it that upset them so much?

I started preaching about the church.

I started talking about how the church is not a program we attend in a building once a week but a life we live every day as we seek to inhabit our neighbourhoods and communities with the love of Jesus.

I also spoke about how there wasn't much value in showing up to our building each week if we weren't seeking to humbly live out God's love every day—and how catching a vision of God's mission for the church would radically change the way we lived and organized ourselves as the church.

I tried to paint a vision of what God really intended for this community called "the church," and about how it was so much bigger and more beautiful (and messier) than what we'd understood it to be.

And that greatly upset some people (while admitting that I'm sure they were also upset by my imperfect delivery of such a message), indicating to me that, perhaps, people didn't actually understand the gospel as well as they thought they did since it became very evident to me that they had put their security in "doing" church a certain way rather than living out the amazing and awesome and spacious freedom God's love gives us.

I thought of all that again as I read Marcos's manuscript. I thought of how people reading this book will be challenged to reframe their understanding of church, which may stretch them a bit.

Marcos writes with such clarity and passion, though—which is amazing and inspiring. He confronts many of our misperceptions, which may border on idolatry at times, and constantly points us to a bolder vision.

And that's precisely the point: Marcos writes with such conviction not because he is pessimistic about the church but because he is so inspired by and optimistic about what the church can and should be.

Simply put, he has a very profound view of the church. He longs for it to step into the fullness of what God designed and longed for it to be.

The church, in truth, could be—and was intended to be—the most beautiful, powerful, loving, inspiring force on earth.

Instead, we've turned it into a very dry, lifeless, judgmental, oppressive institution, more concerned with preserving rituals and traditions than in stepping into the big and spacious mission of God.

Thankfully, wonderfully, Marcos points us to that big and spacious mission, inviting us to join God in what He's already doing in our neighbourhoods and communities, and encouraging us to organize our shared life around community.

In calling us to such a huge vision, Marcos doesn't at all downplay the need to be grounded in Scripture. Indeed, his vision for the church is borne out of his very robust understanding of the biblical narrative, which makes this book all the more powerful.

If your experience is like mine while reading this book, you'll find yourself underlining more sentences than leaving untouched. There were so many times my jaw dropped.

So please read and be challenged.

Ponder it, internalize it, and then—most importantly—live it out!

—Pastor Shawn Brace

CHAPTER 1

MYSTERY

It happened in 2014. Years of dreaming, planning, and working finally came together. The local SDA conference where I lived in Perth, Western Australia gave me a call. They wanted to hire me as a full-time pastoral intern. I accepted in a heartbeat, put my notice in with my employer, and shortly after began a journey that had been years in the making.

Nearly a decade has passed since. I am no longer a pastoral intern. I have since become an ordained minister and worked in diverse churches and districts. At the moment, I am in the midst of leading a missional church planting movement in my city. But that's not all. Over the last decade, I have also hosted an online ministry where I train secular and urban missionaries to share the gospel in contemporary post-church contexts. I host a podcast, post blogs, publish books, have an online training school and a secular outreach Bible study guide all focused on equipping the next generation of missionaries.

The church I planted started with one team in 2019 and launched in 2020. The pandemic season of 2021-22 slowed us down, but despite this, the one team of 12 people has grown to three teams of 65 with over 20 seekers being actively discipled. At the moment of writing two of the three teams are so full we are making plans for multiplication, and another team running a mid-week Bible study for women has had to multiply the study gatherings into three different groups. Best of all, our discipleship pathways are filled with dechurched and unchurched seekers and our missional engagement is one-hundred percent. All of this, while serving in a highly secular, post-religious Australian context.

I don't say all this to self-promote. I say it because I want you to appreciate one simple thing: As a pastor, I have an overwhelming and burning passion. This passion moves me, drives me, and keeps me up at night sometimes. *That passion is the church*.

Next to Jesus and my family, nothing else takes up more of my time, energy, and focus. My career, my online ministry, and my vision for the future all revolve around this often frustrating, always beautiful theme.

And it is because of this great love that I have for the church, for the good news it is called to announce, and for the mission God has given it, that I often find myself challenging, confronting, and calling out the church. I love the church, and at times, love means that I have a moral obligation to contend with the church, to remind it of its high calling, and to resist the missionally corrosive traditions we have become enamoured with.

Encountering The Great Mystery

In this brief book, I would like to do just that. And I want to begin with an odd theme that shows up quite a few times in the New Testament (NT): the theme of *mystery*.

In the book of Ephesians, Paul spends time unpacking this "mystery" that God has had from eternity.

The apostle refers to this mystery as "the mystery made known to me by revelation", "the mystery of Christ which was not made known to people in other generations", and "this mystery, which for ages past was kept *hidden* in God." (Ephesians 3:1-9, *emphasis mine.*)

When you read this, it's obvious whatever Paul is talking about is epic. A mystery kept hidden in God for thousands of years? A mystery only now made known through divine revelation? What could this possibly be?

It reminds me a bit of a TV show called "Blacklist." One of the main characters has a secret and the entire plot is built around that secret. For nine straight seasons, the secret remains hidden. The viewer can only assume and guess what it is. After a 9th season of this, I said to my wife, "They have strung us along with this dumb secret for forever. So, whatever it is, it had better be good."

Well, forget 9 seasons of a TV show (which is roughly equivalent to 9 years). The secret or mystery Paul speaks of in Ephesians has been hidden in God for *thousands* of years. For generations upon generations. It was not revealed to them. Only to us, in these days, has it been made known.

So, what is this mystery Paul speaks of?

In order to fully see it and appreciate it, we need to understand the theme of Ephesians overall. And the theme of Ephesians, it turns out, is built on the ancient story of Israel throughout the Old Testament (OT). Which means we need to go back to Abraham and work our way forward. Only then can we have a proper understanding of what Paul's letter to the Ephesians is truly getting at, and in turn, what Paul means by the term "mystery."

That task is essentially what this whole book is about. But rather than keep you waiting to the end, (like the Blacklist TV series) I am going to jump ahead, tell you exactly what that mystery is, and then unpack it in more depth and detail throughout the rest of the book.

In chapter three of Ephesians, Paul lays this mystery out for us when he says:

> This mystery is that through the gospel the Gentiles are heirs together with Israel, members together of one body, and sharers together in the promise in Christ Jesus.
> —Eph. 3:6, *underline supplied*

Notice Paul's description of "this mystery". He says the mystery is that in Christ, Gentiles and Israel unite as *one*.

Let me add a bit of context now so you can see where Paul is headed.

The story of scripture begins with creation where God makes humanity to be in relationship with him. That story is then interrupted by the fall. Sin creates a wedge, or separation, between God and people. But God has a plan. His plan is that a Messiah will come and restore the human species back into "oneness" with him.

As part of this plan, God calls a man named Abram and tells him that he is going to create a new nation through him. This new nation is the people of Israel, and through this new nation, God will draw all the other nations back to himself.

And now, the promise has come true. Jesus has arrived. His gospel of the Kingdom is a message that in him, he is creating a new humanity that is international. The new nation of Abraham was never meant to be national (Jews only) but the means through which God would regather a family of all nations, tribes, tongues, and people.

That might not seem too crazy in our modern, humanitarian, social justice driven age of inclusivity. But throughout history, national identity has been the primary determinant of who is in and who is out. Even Israel fell into this trap, believing that the promises of God were only for them and that all non-Jews were unclean and forsaken by God.

And now, all of a sudden, Jesus comes along with this radical message that transcends all human categories and breaks down all walls of separation. He praises a centurion, honours a Canaanite, blesses a Samaritan, and embraces the outcast. In him, all are made "one." For Paul, this phenomenon of the "one body" is the mystery that God has kept hidden for generations.

But Paul doesn't stop there. Later in Ephesians 5, he revisits this mystery and clarifies exactly what he is speaking about when he writes:

> This mystery is great, but I speak concerning Christ and <u>the church</u>. (32)

Like I said, we are going to unpack this more as we go. For now, I just wanted to give a bit of context. Because what you are about to see is mind blowing.

Paul says God has a mystery he has kept hidden. That mystery is that in Jesus, all humanity is made "one". This mystery has ancient roots, going all the way back to God's covenant with Abram, and now fulfilled through the death and resurrection of Jesus.

This new nation—the covenant family of the OT—now becomes a new phenomenon in the NT, a divine force that no one saw coming and through which God will usher in a new humanity and a new kingdom on the earth.

And that force, that hidden mystery Paul is speaking of, this radical multi-national family that breaks down every wall of separation and cultivates a new civilisation is none other than (drumroll please): *"the church."*

The church is his mystery. His "one body." His secret weapon. His grand enigma. His new Israel.[1] The thing he kept *hidden*.[2]

Are you blown away? Or disappointed?

I'll be honest with you. I wasn't blown away *or* disappointed when I saw this. The truth is, I didn't even react. I just kind of kept reading and moved on as though nothing had happened. And that is tragic.

---

[1] In this book, the term "New Israel" is employed for the sake of clarity, rather than as an endorsement of supersessionism or replacement theology. See "Appendix C: Israel" for further reading.

[2] It's important to note that the truths of the New Testament already existed in the old. The nation of Israel was the "church" of the Old Testament. Already back then, it was meant to be a nation of priests that welcomed the gentiles into its community. In that sense, the church has always existed. So then, what does Paul mean by referring to this as a mystery? In what sense was it "kept hidden in God?" One possible answer is that God didn't hide it on purpose. He has kept it a secret for centuries, not because he wanted to, but because people kept missing it. Nevertheless, through the full revelation of the gospel and the outpouring of the Spirit post-Calvary, his revelation finally broke through and "turned the world upside-down." (Acts 17:6)

God's mystery of the church, hidden for over four millennia, wasn't capable of eliciting even the slightest emotional reaction from me. Not even a tiny, "*wow*."

Why? Why did the eternal mystery, hidden in the heart of God for centuries and made known—not through human philosophy or insight—but only through miraculous divine revelation, inspire no response in me?

I think the answer is simple. Although I read that the great mystery of God extended to the church, this "one body" Paul spoke of, I honestly had no idea what the church actually was. In my mind, church was an event, a program I attended at a building in town for a few hours on Sabbath where I stood up and sat down at the prescribed moments, kept quiet, listened to a sermon, had some lunch and a few chit-chats, sometimes went for a youth hike after, and then went home.

There was nothing mind-blowing about church. Nothing earth-shattering. For me, it was nice. I enjoyed it. And I especially loved a good sermon. But it was just the same old thing week after week.

If you had asked me to think of a list of words that described the church, I could have chosen many positive terms. But one word I would never have thought of would be "mystery." Why?

Few people have captured the answer to this question as well as pastor and missionary Francis Chan who wrote,

> Church today has become predictable.... You go to a building, someone gives you a bulletin, you sit in a chair, you sing a few songs, a guy delivers maybe a polished message, maybe not,

> someone sings a solo, you go home... Is that all God intended for us?[3]

Chan's words might be unpleasant to those of us who find meaning and value in today's modern church structure and programs, but they are worth considering.

After all, if the mystery hidden for thousands of generations turns out to be nothing more than a blueprint for a Sabbath morning program that we run on repeat week after week then, I must admit, that's a pretty colossal letdown.

Is this the big mystery? Is this what was hidden for so long? Is this the secret plan through which you will flood the earth with your glory?

Pews and lecterns? Suits and ties? 3-hymn sandwiches and a weekly Bible lecture?

The same old program, in the same old format, year after year?

Is this what you had in mind as you delivered Israel, conquered Canaan, toppled giants, and rained fire from heaven?

That all that stuff was just a pre-cursor, a taste of a grand mystery to come that would change the course of history, and it turns out the grand mystery is a formal program complete with a formal British parliamentary dress code, a minute by minute outline, and a list of songs we sing half asleep?

---

[3] Kwon, Lilian. "Francis Chan: Church Today Not What God Intended," (Web: christianpost.com)

Is the big mystery that God would load up on real estate, so we could build permanent structures that are empty six days a week?

Is the hidden thing a series of programs where 80% of the attendees never participate but only spectate?

Is the big mystery that pastors would be burned out with endless committees, long business meetings arguing about carpets, and board meetings burdened by the stresses of bills, finances, insurance and building repairs?

I don't know you guys. Say whatever you want, flip and twist and spin as much as you like. You can call the above scenario—a script of most of our modern-day churches—anything you want. But DON'T call it a *mystery*.

It's not.

And this is why Paul's words in Ephesians didn't excite me or even offend me. Because when I read that the mystery was God bringing all people together into one body, I immediately knew Paul was speaking of the church. And when I thought "church", I thought about the nice little program I attend every weekend. And my mind just could not fathom how that formulaic event could possibly encapsulate anything close to a mystery.

And here's the real reason why: *I had no idea what the church was*. I had attended church events all my life. I had done Bible studies and Sabbath school. I had heard sermons and been through Pathfinders. I had preached and taught and served. I had even accepted a call to be a pastor. And I had no idea what the church really was.

For me, church was a building with a program that I went to. That was the crux of it. And that building with that program took so much of my energy and focus, it made it virtually impossible for me to truly understand the breadth, the depth, the beauty, the glory and the mystery of what the Bible meant when it said, “church.”

It would be another decade before I caught my first glimpse of the eternal mystery God had in mind.

CHAPTER 2

TEMPLE

Before we can appreciate what the mystery God had in mind (the church) actually is, we need to spend some time clearing the air. Because it turns out there are so many myths and misconceptions about what the church is, that unless we declutter all that noise it's not possible to fully appreciate the biblical picture. So, for the next few chapters we are going to slowly deconstruct the modern conception of church so that in the end, we can appreciate the depth of its mystery with awe.

When it comes to defining what the church is NOT, most people nowadays quickly jump on the "church is not a building" line.

Now, they aren't wrong. In fact, I am one of them. Here, let me go ahead and repeat it:

The church is NOT a building.

But this oft-repeated statement has one major flaw. All it does is tell us the church is NOT a building. What it fails to capture is that the church is much more than NOT a building. It is literally counter-building. In other words, the NT church isn't just standing on the side of the road saying, "I am not a building!" It's actually on the road, running in the opposite direction.

Some people think the early church had no buildings because they were still working on their deposit. I have even had people tell me that if given the chance, they are sure the early Christians would have built church buildings like ours. In this sense, they fail to see that the NT church isn't merely NOT a building. It is actively, intentionally, and purposefully going in the opposite direction of a building.

When I share this, however, some point to Jesus' custom of attending Synagogue or the presence of a physical temple in Israel as evidence that having a church building is central to God's plan for his church. But all this shows is how shallow our theology of church really is. To compare the eternal mystery God had kept secret for thousands of years with a Synagogue (which was basically a community centre for Jewish religious and social life) and the OT temple (which met its end at the death of Jesus and played a role completely different to the church) is to reveal how elementary our biblical understanding of church really is.

> But the early church met in homes and homes are buildings, therefore buildings are part of the church's biblical DNA.

Yep, some folks have said this to me. But if we stick to scripture alone, you'll soon see the Bible has a different picture it is inviting us to see.

For starters, it doesn't take a lot of thoughtful energy to know there is a massive difference between someone's home and a building—especially the kinds of church buildings we have today, which look and function entirely different to the simple homes of first-century believers.

Second, just read the Bible. The word church appears 114 times in the NT. Not once does it refer to a building. Every single time it refers to people. The church, then, is not an IT but an US. It is not a place you attend, but an identity you embrace. We don't go to church; we ARE the church.

In fact, the Greek word we translate as "church" is "*ekklesia*" which has a handful of different meanings such as "a gathering", "an assembly", or "called out." In other words, the church in the NT is a gathering and coming together of people who have been called out of the fallen nations, empires, and hierarchical ways of thinking and into a new family and civilisation that loves like Jesus.

Of course, this gathering can take place in a building. But don't let that trick you into thinking our modern way of using buildings is somehow justified or healthy. The bottom line is, the church can gather anywhere, but it is not defined by its "where" so much as it's defined by its "who."

So even though a church can gather in a building, it is not tied to one, dependent on one, nor defined by one. The early church met primarily in homes, but we also see them gathering in the marketplace, in the Synagogues and Temple courts and in their neighbourhoods. This decentralised movement wasn't a holdover while they waited on a property loan. The non-building centric nature of the NT was intentional.

What The Church Is

The best way to begin grasping the deep mystery of the church is to follow the story of scripture. I am going to assume the reader is familiar with the Great Controversy theme, so I won't go into creation, the fall and God's desire to restore us to relationship with himself. Instead, I want to skip ahead to the sanctuary which God told the people of Israel to build so that he could "dwell among them." (Exodus 25:8)

In the OT, God's presence inhabited this sanctuary. The original design (which eventually became the temple in Israel) was mobile, not stationary. And God's presence dwelled in this space. The meaning communicated here cannot be overlooked. The sanctuary in scripture represents God's desire to be *with* people. Almost as if he created us to be intimate cosmic neighbours. Sin damaged the neighbourhood and introduced distance, separation, and broken relationship.

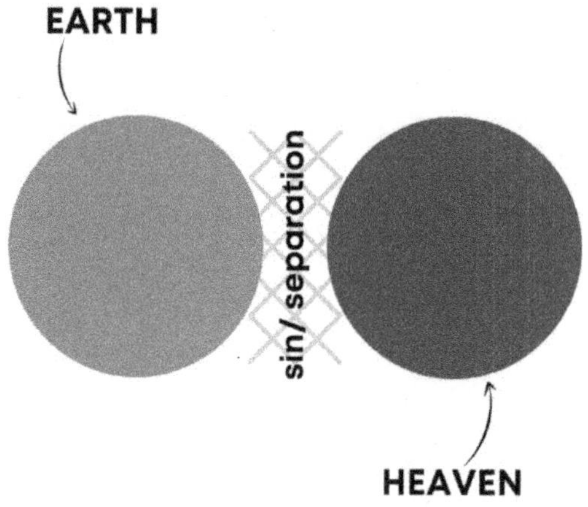

However, in the sanctuary, we find a God who shows up with a plan to repair the broken neighbourhood. At the centre of this plan is his obvious longing to be close to us. This is why Gabriel announced that the saviour would be called "Immanuel" which means "God with us." (Matthew 1:23) John also describes Jesus in John 1 as the word who "became flesh and dwelt among us." The Greek word for "dwelt" in this passage literally means "to pitch one's tent." In other words, Jesus is God who moved into our neighbourhood and pitched his tent among us—the ultimate manifestation of the sanctuary in the OT.

For this reason, the sanctuary is depicted throughout scripture as a space where heaven and earth meet. If you can picture heaven as a circle and earth as a circle, the two are separated by sin. But in the sanctuary (or temple), the two separate dimensions overlap.

Jefferson Bethke described this brilliantly as "the place where heaven and earth collide."[4] God's Spirit is in there and if someone wanted to encounter God, they would go to the temple where the dimension of fallen man touched the dimension of God's presence. This metaphysical space then became the gate through which the two separated dimensions could once again be one, despite the presence of sin.

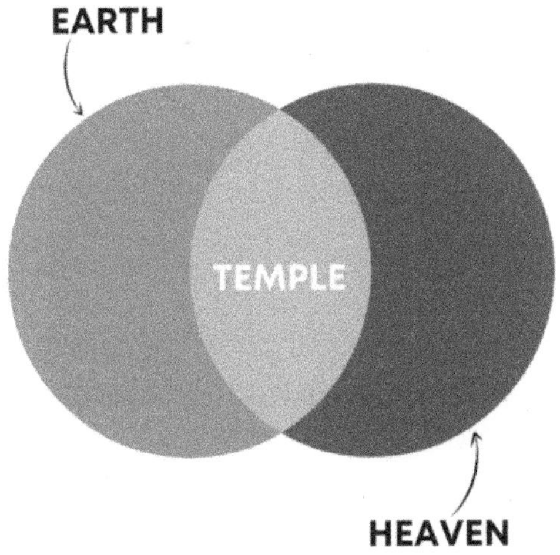

In the NT, the earthly temple meets its end at the death of Jesus.

Why? Because the sin that causes separation between earth and heaven has been conquered by Jesus. The promises and symbols in the sanctuary all pointed to him and have now been fulfilled. So, the earthly sanctuary/temple ceases to be the interdimensional embassy between heaven and earth.

[4] See Bethke, Jefferson. "It's Not What You Think" (Thomas Nelson Publishers, 2015)

However, the Great Controversy isn't over yet. Sin is still here. Heaven is still out there. Humanity still requires a meeting ground that connects heaven to earth. So, if the temple is finished, what takes its place?

Paul answers this question for us when he writes to the believers,

> Don't you know that you yourselves are God's temple and that God's Spirit dwells in you? (1 Corinthians 3:16)

Did you catch that? I hope so because something radically insane has taken place. Because of the gospel, God now does a new thing. He births his desired temple, not with some new and fancy building, but with people. *With you, and with me.* We, fallen but redeemed, broken but restored, sinful but reborn—full of scars and weaknesses and frailties—*WE* are now the temple.

In other words, God doesn't transfer the sanctity of the OT temple to a new edifice called the "church." Instead, he transfers the sanctity of the OT temple to people. Human beings now become walking temples. They become, collectively as a people, the space where heaven and earth collide.

This means that you, we as believers in Jesus, are filled with the Spirit of God just like the OT temple, thus making us not merely church members, but a walking multidimensional embassy of heaven.

Earth and heaven literally collide in you and me, not merely in an individual sense, but in a collective, unified sense. This means that if someone wants to encounter the presence of

God, they no longer need to go to a permanent structure in Israel. God has done something insane. He has flooded the earth with mini-temples of his Spirit to the degree that when people enter the relational perimeter of our homes, lives, and community they enter into a mini-temple space where heaven and earth meet. And like the original sanctuary, like the throne of God with wheels in Ezekiel's vision, these mini-temples are mobile.

They are EVERYWHERE.

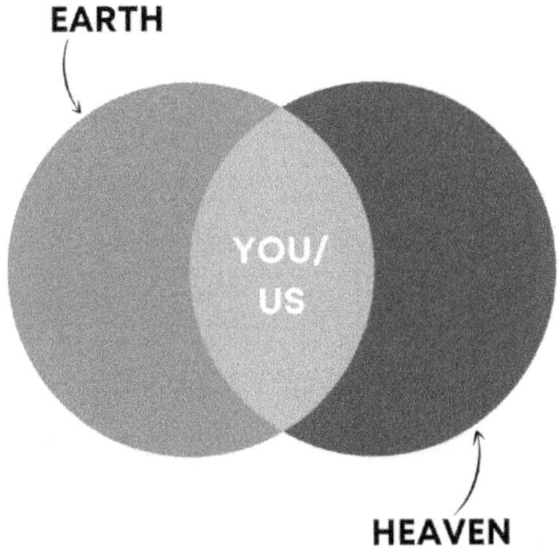

The NT church, then, is a gathered and scattered movement of people filled with the Spirit of God who are not restrained by permanent structures but free to move in and through society. And Satan was taken by surprise. The OT might have featured a central temple that contained the presence of God, but now the temple has been decentralised. *It is everywhere.* Everyday people all throughout the city have now become habitations of the Spirit's supernatural presence.

While the enemy focused his attacks on destroying the temple in the OT, in the NT he could no longer do this. Instead, he finds himself disoriented and scrambling to push back against the new thing God is doing. Why? Because the NT temple was everywhere. In homes, parks, and marketplaces. In the temple courts, Synagogues, and street corners. It was no longer restrained to one central location. It was everywhere, and it was so powerful the church became known as the people who "turned the world upside down." (Acts 17:6)

No buildings. No professional clergy. No microphones, projectors, or bands. No multi-million-dollar complexes. None of the stuff we think we need today. And yet, they up-ended society.

What Changed?

Today we have millions of dollars' worth of resources and buildings. But the weird thing is, our churches are struggling to reach their communities. What happened? How did the church that once turned the world upside down become so ineffective?

I think a better question to ask is: How would Satan respond to this new, unexpected mobile, mini-temple threat? He tried social pressure and that didn't work. He tried persecution, imprisonment, and even death. That didn't work either. So, what could he do?

I'll tell you what I would do. If I were leading a war against God, and he showed up with this secret weapon of mini-temples flooding the earth, I would put all my energy into reversing the spread of these mini-temples. But I wouldn't do it via persecution because, for some reason, that just causes the church to grow more. No, if I were the devil, I would have to disarm this new movement with something way more subtle.

Rather than persecution and bloodshed, I would offer them comfort. I would sneakily draw them into big, centralised buildings that host spiritual programs few ever participate in and which, while enjoyable and nice, keep them spiritually cosy and unaware of the radical vision God has in mind for them.

And this is precisely what has happened. Forgive my direct language here, I don't intend to be callous, only brief. Today, many churches function like clubs. They offer a certain brand of religious programming and just enough semblances of success to keep us content—with the feeling that we are doing something when the truth is, we are asleep.

Few of us ever reach another person for Christ. Few of us ever use our gifts to build the Kingdom. Few of us can share our faith winsomely or know how to bless others, how to give a Bible study, how to be agents of healing in our spheres of influence, or how to contextualise the good news of Jesus in order to reach new generations. Few of us know what our spiritual gifts are. Deacons have become clean-up crews. Elders have become program managers. Pastors have become committee administrators. In many of our churches, relationships end the moment people walk out the front door. There is little true community. We do not love one another deeply, and all it takes is the slightest disagreement—like changing the colour of the carpet or installing a projector—to have us at each other's throats.

We are no longer living as disciple-makers, missionaries, ambassadors, or a kingdom of priests leading all within our reach to an encounter with the heart of God. Instead, we live as members of spiritual clubs that promise to cater to our needs with well-designed, well-executed programs and events.

We don't gather to be equipped for intentional and effective mission. Instead, we have a spiritual booster shot every weekend with sermons we can hardly remember two days later, let alone share. In fact, I would say that most of our weekend church services are not really booster shots as much as they are sedatives. The nice program with the good sermon and the predictable traditions isn't really designed to empower us, it's designed to keep us content and coming back for more. And what about mission? We leave that to the missionaries. Justice? We leave that to ADRA. Evangelism? We leave that to the international speakers with the big budgets.

Wrapping Up

Satan's tactic reminds me a lot of the drug cartels. A cartel's main job is to get drugs from one location to another to maximise sales and profit. The last thing they want is for their drug shipment to be discovered and turned over to the police. However, they are happy for the police to catch a drug shipment worth hundreds of thousands if it means that, as the police celebrate their awesome catch, the cartel's real shipment (worth millions) sneaks by undetected.

It's a classic distraction strategy. "We will sacrifice this shipment to make you feel like you are doing something. And as you celebrate, we sneak underneath with the real shipment and make our millions."

Satan has us relaxed. Our programs are just good enough. Our baptism numbers are just good enough. Our success is just good enough. Enough for us to celebrate while he sneaks by the church to draw the city and culture we inhabit further and further from God.

Sure, go ahead and baptise ten. And in the meantime, I'll destroy thousands.

His main tool to keep this strategy working? Lull the church to sleep with endless programs, endless events, endless retreats, endless repetition, endless tradition, and endless consumer driven spectator services where 80% of the people will never use the radical power available to them via the indwelling of the Spirit because all they ever do is observe a program put on by professionals.

So here is my conclusion. The church is NOT a building, but it is more than NOT a building. It runs in the opposite direction to a building. It is a radical movement of human mini-temples flooding the earth with God's glory, sneaking into every crevice and nook of society with the healing power of the gospel, unrestrained and free to move—just like Jesus. And if I were the devil, the first thing I would do to fight back would be to "de-scatter" the mini-temples and siphon them into one central location where I can pacify them with endless programming, occupy them with bills, maintenance and overhead, and get most of the congregation to never use their Spiritual gifts. In doing so, perhaps they will lose sight of whom they truly are and settle for something less.

But the amazing news is, God's truth can't be contained or deleted. As we begin to rediscover, individually and collectively, our identity as human mini-temples whose calling it is to bring heaven to earth, we will begin to see an awakening of radical proportions. No longer restrained by real estate and property boundaries, we will at last claim our place at the table of our neighbourhoods.

CHAPTER 3

HOUSE

Before I tell you what the church is not, I have to warn you, this chapter might be a bit uncomfortable. But, before you head to my DMs to declare war, make sure you read the whole thing.

Ok, you have been warned. So here we go: In the previous chapter we saw that the church is not a building. Equally important is to come to this realisation:

The church building that we attend every Sabbath is NOT the "house of God."

I hear it all the time in every church I attend. In fact, I have heard this my entire life. People point to the church building and refer to it as the "temple" or the "sanctuary" or the "house of the Lord."

In fact, preachers often quote David at the start of the church service saying, "I was glad when they said, let us go into the house of the Lord." (Psalm 122:1)

And of course, every pastor knows that one of the most stressful things to manage is "reverence" in the church. People come out with all kinds of quotes about how the temple, sanctuary or house of God should be reverenced. In the church I grew up in, deacons would hand a card with Habakkuk 2:20 to anyone who was making noise during the service:

> The LORD is in his holy temple; let all the earth be silent before him.

The idea that the church building *is* the temple, the sanctuary or the house of God is deeply rooted in most modern Christianity—and certainly in Adventism. Even Adventist pioneer Ellen G White referred to the church building as "the house of God" and "the sanctuary for the congregation." (BTW, I touch on this in Appendix A)

But here is the truth, you guys. If you stick to the story of scripture, you can't get away from the fact that the building on the street corner where we run religious programs is NOT the "house of the Lord." Not even close.

But how can I make such a radical claim?

Let's find out.

What The Church Is

The best way to appreciate all this, is to, once again, follow the story of scripture and allow it to speak to us. So, let's go back to the OT, particularly Exodus 25:8 which says:

> Have them make a sanctuary for me, and I will dwell among them.

Notice this: God wants his people to build him a sanctuary. His promise is that he wants to live, or "dwell", among his people.

Since God is going to dwell in this structure, it is obviously a "dwelling place" for God. In a sense, you could say that the OT sanctuary is going to be the "house of God."

Now, I don't know about you, but if I was told to build a house for God my imagination would go wild with how epic this thing is going to look.

And yet, when God gives the instructions, we don't get epic.

In fact, we get the opposite.

The instructions are basically a blueprint for a *tent*.

Are you serious? Does this look like the dwelling place for the creator of the universe? A tent?

Yep. That's it. It's not a castle. It's not a Taj Mahal. It's not a palace. *It's a tent*. A plain, humble, small-looking tent.

And God liked his tent. Exodus 40:34 tells us that "the glory of the Lord filled" it with fire which appears to be God's way of saying, "yep, I'm totally digging this."

But then something happened. A twist in the story. And this twist is so twisty that unless we untwist it, we will continue to have a flawed, anorexic view of what the church is.

Here's what happened: King David was sitting in his fancy palace one day (never a good thing for David to be doing), and he had a thought. *Why do I get to sit in this nice palace while God lives in a tent? This isn't cool. I'm going to make God a nice house.*

Very sweet of ol' David. But God doesn't seem to be into it. Instead, he replies:

> I have never lived in a house... My home has always been a tent, moving from one place to

> another... I have never once complained [or asked] "Why haven't you built me a beautiful house?" (1 Chronicles 17: 4-6)

Pay special attention to what God is telling David here. It's pretty straight forward:

I don't want a fancy house.

Could it get any clearer? But God goes on, in verse 11 he adds:

> When you die and join your ancestors, I will raise up one of your descendants, one of your sons, and I will make his kingdom strong. He is the one who will build a house—a temple—for me. And I will secure his throne forever.... I will confirm him as king over my house and my kingdom for all time, and his throne will be secure forever. (1 Chronicles 17:10-12, 14)

Notice what God says here. I'm going to break this down so it's super simple to follow:

1. God doesn't want David to build him a permanent house.
2. However, God does admit that from David's dynasty, there will come a descendant—a son of David—and this son is the one who will build a house for God.

Now in case you have gotten to this part of the chapter, and you are starting to wonder where in the world this is all headed and why you should care—I have to tell you, it's about to get way worse. Because it's here, at this point in the story, where things get weird.

And the weirdness revolves around one central question:

Who is this "son" God is speaking about?

Is it David's firstborn son, *Solomon*?

Or is it a descendant later down the line? (Like, maybe *Jesus*? Here's a cute little image to make this part easier to grasp :

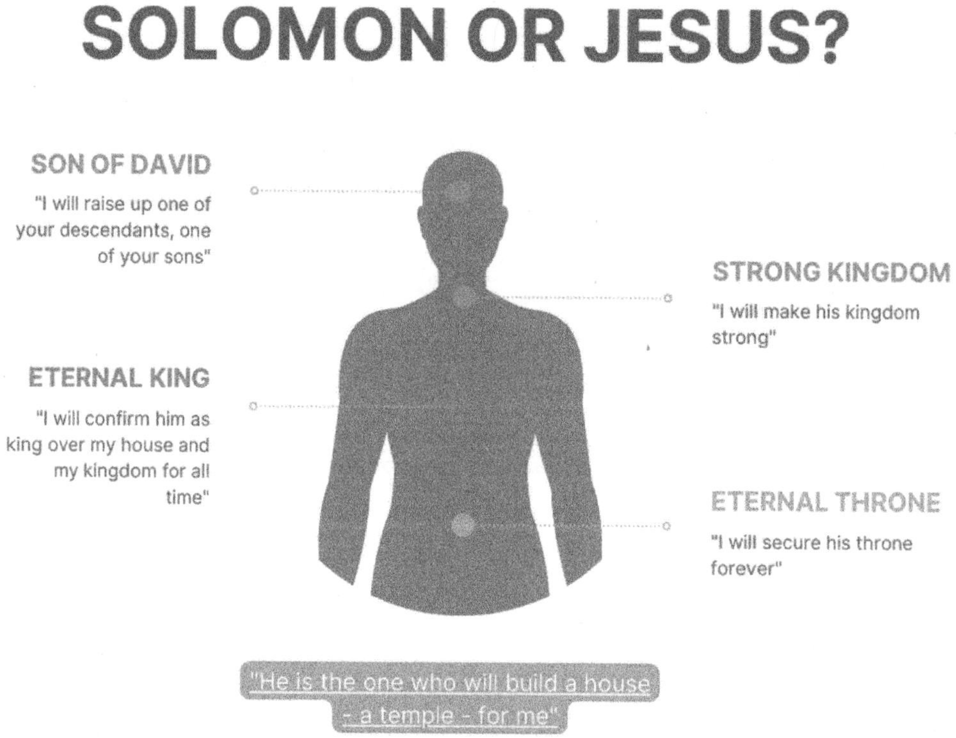
SOLOMON OR JESUS?
SON OF DAVID
"I will raise up one of your descendants, one of your sons"
STRONG KINGDOM
"I will make his kingdom strong"
ETERNAL KING
"I will confirm him as king over my house and my kingdom for all time"
ETERNAL THRONE
"I will secure his throne forever"
"He is the one who will build a house - a temple - for me"

Solomon seems to tick two out of the four boxes. He was definitely one of David's kids. And Israel was arguably strong under Solomon. In fact, people came from different nations to check out all the cool stuff Israel was up to under Solomon.

However, Solomon doesn't tick the last two boxes (more on this later).

So again, I ask, who is the "son" God is speaking of?

At the risk of being annoying let me repeat myself. If we say the "son" God spoke of is David's firstborn son (Solomon), we run into a problem. God said this "son" who would "build me a house" would be king over God's house *for all time*. This is an *eternal king*, with an *eternal kingship*. And none of David's kids match this description—not even Solomon.

The only "son of David" who does match this description is *Jesus*.

Why does this matter?

You are about to find out why. But hang in there. Remember, we are untwisting some pretty twisty stuff here. So don't fall asleep. It's all about to come together and what you are going to see is going to rock your world big time.

However, I totally get that by this point your brain might be in need of a break. So, I'm going to insert those mysterious little asterisks below which basically imply "take a break here." Have a stretch, enjoy a hot chocolate, watch some TikTok videos, and then come back, ready to experience something epic.

***

When you left, we were trying to figure out who the son God spoke of to David (the one who would build God's house) is.

Could it be Solomon?

Or someone else, like Jesus?

And why does any of this even matter?

So far, we have seen that Solomon doesn't match the description given by God.[5] Only one "son of David" in history does—and it's Jesus.

Now, of course, it's perfectly possible to suggest the vision was talking about both Solomon and Jesus. Visions in the Bible have dual-applications all the time. Solomon could represent a failed human attempt at the temple, and Jesus would then serve as a divine contrast that brings in the authentic thing—the true temple God always wanted. Alternatively, the vision might have had nothing to do with Solomon at all. These two options are both feasible, but here is my point: Although the vision could refer to A) both Solomon and Jesus, or B) only Jesus, there is no way the vision refers to Solomon alone. At best, Solomon is on the periphery—a thin shadow of what is to come that ends in failure and catastrophe. He was never meant to be the fulfilment of this vision in any central or cosmic sense.

But David didn't know this. And can we blame him? Humans have always struggled to see the full picture that God is up to. And as we have already seen, God's full picture was a mystery only fully revealed in the NT. So, it's no wonder then, that David believes the vision is about Solomon. He even gives a speech before his death in which he says God told him Solomon was the temple builder (even though Solomon was never named by God). So, after David's death, Solomon becomes king. And of

---

[5] The only text that seems to strongly imply Solomon as the object of the prophecy is 2 Samuel 7:14 which says, "*If he commits iniquity*, I will chasten him with the rod of men, and with the stripes of the children of men." (*Italics supplied*) I explore this text in more detail in Appendix B.

course, Solomon believes *he is the son* who will build God's house. So, he sends a letter to the king of Tyre and tells him,

> I intend to build a temple for the Name of the Lord my God, as the Lord told my father David, when he said, "Your son whom I will put on the throne in your place will build the temple for my Name." (1 Kings 5:5)

Solomon thinks *he is the son* God spoke of because the poor guy has no idea that God was speaking of Jesus. So, with this twisty idea in his mind, the king gets to work, building a temple God never asked for. And like David, Solomon is thinking of a permanent and fancy structure.

What happened next is nothing short of tragic. Solomon raised taxes considerably for the construction of the new, magnificent temple. The finished product was an impressive sight to behold. But the people were not happy. When Solomon died, his son Rehoboam was to take the throne. But the people of Israel were fed up with the endless labour and heavy taxes it took for Solomon to build his fancy temple. They said to Rehoboam,

> Your father was a hard master... Lighten the harsh labour demands and heavy taxes that your father imposed on us. Then we will be your loyal subjects. (1 Kings 12:4)

Rehoboam refused. And from that moment forward, the kingdom of Israel began to crumble. The dynasty of David collapsed. The nation split into the northern and southern kingdoms until the northern was dispersed and the southern was taken captive.

It's clear that Solomon was not the promised son who would build God's house. The promised son, God said, would have a strong kingdom, an eternal throne, an eternal kingdom, and an eternal kingship. If anything, Solomon was the antithesis of all this. Through his pride and arrogance, his lust for elegance and prestige, Solomon set in motion the eventual collapse of Israel.

Enter Jesus...

But the story isn't over yet. Jesus arrives in the NT. He is the son of David—the promised one whose throne would endure forever. The one who would build God's house.

But then another weird thing happens. When Jesus dies, he brings an end to the temple's function and purpose. The curtain is torn in two, signifying the temple's end. So, rather than build God's house, Jesus seems to do the opposite. *He appears to destroy it.*

However, the above is only true if we assume that the permanent temple *is* God's house. *But it's not.*

Jesus has come to build the true house God wants, and he begins by cancelling the temple. This is no longer the place where the fire dwells. This is no longer God's house. In fact, it was never meant to be. A new one—the true one—is coming.

It All Happens in the Book of Acts...

After his resurrection, Jesus tells his disciples to go to Jerusalem and wait for the outpouring of his Spirit. He returns to heaven, and as the disciples are waiting in a house, something remarkable happens:

> Suddenly a sound like the blowing of a violent wind came from heaven and filled the whole house where they were sitting. They saw what seemed to be tongues of fire that separated and came to rest on each of them. All of them were filled with the Holy Spirit... (Acts 1:1-4)

Did you notice it? The disciples are all in a house in Jerusalem. And while they are there, the Holy Spirit is poured out and the presence of God fills "the whole house." And just as in the OT Temple, the presence is identified by fire.

As pastor Ivor Myers said in his sermon, "Housefires" (the inspiration for this whole chapter by the way) – "Fire filled the house."

Can you see how radical that is? "The glory of the Lord filled" the house with "fire." The same fire that filled the OT sanctuary with the glory of God now fills a random house with dusty floors, snotty kids, and dirty towels.

Don't miss the significance of this. In the OT, the temple was filled with the supernatural fire of God's holy presence. In the NT, the same fire fills—not a new permanent building somewhere in the centre of town—but a plain old house.

And notice this other verse from Acts. Having just been released from custody, Peter and John meet with the other believers in an undisclosed location (most likely a house) for a prayer meeting. While they were praying the text says,

> ...the place was shaken where they were gathered together. (Acts 4:31)

A place shaking because God's presence is there? While God-earthquakes are a theme that pops up quite a bit in scripture, two specific instances connect deeply with the experience in Act's. The first is God's presence on Mount Sainai (Exodus 19:18) which caused the mountain to tremble, and the second is Isaiahs's vision of God's throne room, where "the foundations of the thresholds shook" (Isaiah 6:4).

Clearly God is up to something radical. And simple, humble homes are at the heart of it.

Why? Because it was ALWAYS meant to be this way. Because this temple, made up of everyday people in everyday homes, this is the temple that God wants. This is the temple he foretold the son of David would build. *Not a temporary temple of brick and wood—an eternal temple of people and homes.*

To be continued...

CHAPTER 4

FIRE

A temple of people and homes. That's the temple God has always wanted. The one he foretold David's descendant would build for him. Not a stationary and fancy structure but a simple and mobile one. You. Me. And the unassuming contours of our homes.

All through the book of Acts, we see the temple growing, not through the construction of centralised mega-churches, cathedrals, or church buildings, but through the fire of that simple, unknown house in Jerusalem spreading to other simple, unknown houses. The temple constructed by the son of David, then, was not a permanent building with stained-glass windows. It was people living all throughout the city, gathering in homes filled with the fire.

The house of God, then, is not a special location separate from everyday existence. The true house of God is a community of people anywhere and everywhere.

This is why Stephen, commenting on the story of Solomon and the temple, declared,

> Solomon built the Temple for God. However, the Most High does not dwell in houses made by human hands. As the prophet said, "Heaven is

> my throne, and the earth is my footstool. What kind of house will you build for me? says the Lord. Or where will my resting place be?" (Acts 7:48-49)

Stephen never answers the question. But later, Peter—borrowing the analogy of a literal building—gives us the answer to God's question:

> And you are living stones that God is building into his spiritual temple. (1 Peter 2:5)

Did you see it?

The house God spoke to David about, the one his offspring (the eternal king, Jesus) would build for him, was not the permanent Solomonic temple, or a church building made of brick and drywall—but a spiritual temple whose walls are made of "living stones" (people) and whose foundation is "the living stone"—Christ himself.[6]

This is the only true dwelling place the eternal, transcendent God has ever really wanted.

All scripture points to and orbits this central theme—and the mystery of Jesus is its fullest articulation on the earth. He was God made man who "dwelt among us" (John 1:14) and through whom the church was birthed. And the church, as his body on

---

[6] Throughout Christian history, there exists a long and convoluted history of anti-Semitic theology. Within this historical context, one encounters anti-Jewish sentiments that contend against the construction of the Old Testament Temple. These perspectives frequently advocate for a supersessionist outlook on the church, a position (as previously stated) not endorsed here. See Appendix C for more information.

earth, is itself an extension of this mystery as the Spirit of God dwells in us, a people.

So as these early believers gathered in that home in Jerusalem, *the fire of God's presence fell upon it.*

Then it spread to another house, and another, and still another.

God's great mystery, hidden in his heart for thousands of years, was not a centralised building with special programs, but an omnipresent temple reclaiming the world home by home, community by community, family by family.

This omnipresent temple began in that unknown house in Jerusalem, and before long the fire spread everywhere.

The world was turned upside down.

What Happened?

The answer to this is complex.[7] For now, I'll simply say this: When centralised church buildings entered the picture the emphasis moves from local houses and everyday people spreading fire throughout their cities to a centralised church building where people come to observe one specially ordained priest or specially chosen choir put on a spiritual show for them week after week. And as this became the norm, the fire died out.

Over time, the Biblical picture of an omnipresent temple reclaiming the earth was lost. The temple moved from a socially present phenomenon to a spiritual castle removed from the rhythms of life's messiness. And with this shift, the mystery of

[7] For a more thorough treatment on this topic, see: Viola, Frank. "Pagan Christianity?: Exploring the Roots of Our Church Practices."

the church moved from this transportable, uncontainable movement spreading fire throughout the city to a static, easily restrained building with a program.

Today, church is essentially that—a pallid and pale version of its true self. A mystery of wonder reduced to a commodity that we can easily compartmentalise into the building over there with the program on that day, which we erroneously refer to as the "house of God." But it's not his house. Not even close. Because God never asked for permanent church buildings. The temple Jesus built and continues to build is a spiritual temple, a spiritual underground of living stones: people, homes, and communities gathered around tables, dirty dishes, noisy kids and the glorious, sacred elegance of the Fire.

Conclusion

As I close this chapter, I want to return to God's message to David in 1 Chronicles 17. Only this time, I want to re-write the text based on the revelation we now have in Jesus, which David did not possess. With Jesus as the interpretive lens, the words of 1 Chronicles 17 come to life, challenging, and inspiring the church today:

> I have never lived in a *church building*; from the day I birthed the *church* at Pentecost until this very day. My *church* has always been a people, moving from one home to another... Yet no matter where I have gone with this people, I have never once complained to the leaders, the shepherds of my *church*. I have never asked them, 'Why haven't you built me a beautiful *church building*?'

Jesus has built me a house—a temple—not of brick and stone, but of lives and homes. He is the living stone and the people, mini 'living stones' that, together, form my true, spiritual temple filling the whole earth. This whole earth belongs to Jesus and is the inheritance of his people. Theirs is a new kingdom and his throne will endure forever.

CHAPTER 5

GLORY

Before we move on from Solomon, there is something I need to show you. It's going to shock you, but it's necessary, so hang in there. I promise, in the end it will have been totally worth it.

Once again, we begin with that famous text:

> Have them make a sanctuary for me, and I will dwell among them. (Exodus 25:8)

Notice God told the people to make him a sanctuary, and then he gave them a set of instructions on how to build the sanctuary. Interestingly, "sanctuary's", "temples", "sacrificial sites" etc. were common in the ancient world Moses inhabited.

However, while the sanctuary had some similarities with these other sites (ex. animal sacrifices, altars, incense etc.), it also had some key differences:

PAGAN TEMPLES	GOD'S SANCTUARY
Buildings	A Tent
Permanent, Location Bound	Mobile, Can Go Anywhere
Fancy	Simple

Situated On Hill, Mountaintops or "High Places"	Situated On Level Ground, In the Middle of Camp
Institutional Injustice Was Always Near	Justice Was Central

By now, you should be familiar with the first three points, so allow me to make some quick comments about the last two: Mountaintops and Justice.

Mountaintops

A common theme we find in the OT when it comes to Pagan temples or shrines is that they are always situated in the "high places." (2 Kings 17:29) We see this repeatedly in Kings and Chronicles. (1 Kings 3:2-3, 13:33, 14:23) Whenever a faithful King came to power, he would get rid of the "high places." (2 Kings 18:4) This is significant because pagan temples were often situated on high ground—on top of hills or mounts. There was a sense in which, to enter the assembly of the gods, one had to go *up* to them.

However, the God of Israel did not demand his people go up to him. Rather, he came *down* to them. As a result, the sanctuary was built on level ground in the midst of the people, in the centre of the Israelite camp. This communicates a very different picture to the pagan model. The God of Israel came down to his people. He was a relational and communal God—his posture was one of divine neighbour.

Justice

Another feature we see repeatedly through the OT is that pagan worship is almost always associated with social injustice.

Pagan prostitution and child sacrifice are some of the more glaring examples. Contrary to popular belief, these were not merely cruel acts practised by uncivilized people. No, the prostitution, orgies, and sacrifices of these ancient groups were features of complex social codes, religious filigrees, mythical cosmologies and, above all, institutional structures at the centre of their societies. All of this coalesced into a kind of systemic and structural oppression that exploited women, children, and captives of war from generation to generation. And this oppressive order was deeply influenced by the gods being worshipped at these temples and shrines.

This is why, whenever Israel begins to worship false gods in the OT stories, we see a quick decline in social, judicial, and humanitarian justice.

To the contrary, the apex of the OT sanctuary was the "Day of Atonement," a day in which Israel as a collective society would cleanse themselves of wrongdoing and be reharmonized to the social code God had given them—a code that included justice for the marginalized. Anyone who refused to participate in the ceremony was removed from the nation altogether. To this day, Jewish people see a very strong relationship between Yom Kippur and human rights.[8]

By now you are probably thinking, "This is cool and all, but where's all the shocking stuff you said you were going to show me? I'm ready for some drama!"

Well, you're in luck. Allow me to now introduce you to shock numero uno.

---

[8] 2023 Union for Reform Judaism. "Yom Kippur Social Action Guide", (Web: reformjudaism.org)

Shock Numero Uno

As we saw in the previous chapters, David wanted to build God a temple. God said *no*. But God also told David that one of his descendants (Jesus) would build him a temple for all time. David thought God meant one of his soon-to-be-born kids. And why not? David wasn't fully aware of the grandeur that God was up to. He was thinking small, not cosmically. So, he automatically assumed one of his kids was the promised Temple-builder. It's no surprise then, that when Solomon comes on the scene, he thinks that he is the guy and immediately got to work on the temple he believed he was meant to build.

And here we run into our first shock of the hour: When Solomon builds his temple, it resembles—not the tent of meeting God instructed Moses to build—but the pagan temples from the surrounding nations. Don't believe me? Just look at the chart:

PAGAN TEMPLES	GOD'S SANCTUARY	SOLOMON'S
Buildings	A Tent	Building
Permanent	Mobile	Permanent
Fancy	Simple	Fancy
Situated on a Hill, "High Places" or Mountaintops	Situated on level ground, in the middle of camp	Situated on a Mountain (Mount Moriah)
Institutional Injustice was Always Near	Justice was Central	Institutional Injustice was Always Near

Once again, let me focus on those last two.

Mountain

Notice that the temple Solomon built was no longer level ground in the centre of the camp of Israel. It was now on mount Moriah. (2 Chronicles 3:1) For the first time in Israelite history, people had to "go up" to meet with God. He was no longer "among" them in the same way. He was now further removed, away from the neighbourhood, and on top of a mountain—just like the pagan temples.

Now let's get something clear here: the idea or image of God residing on a mountain is not pagan in itself. The Bible tells us that the Lord dwells in his "holy mountain" also known as Mount Zion. (Joel 3:17) God also gave his law upon a mountain top (Mount Sinai) and the prophet Micah, speaking of the end of time, says, "It shall come to pass in the latter days that the mountain of the house of the Lord shall be established as the highest of the mountains, and it shall be lifted up above the hills..." (Micah 4:1)

The difference is that while God is depicted as residing on a mountaintop—far above the dwelling place of humanity—he is paradoxically depicted as coming down to dwell among us. In other words, he is transcendent, but he is also immanent. He is far above and beyond us, but he also comes close to dwell among us. This is the difference between the pagan cosmology and the Hebraic. In scripture, God does not give us a list of rules to follow so we can reach the mountaintop where he is. Instead, he comes down and dwells among us in order to bring us to his mountain through relationship. Isaiah captures this vision multiple times when he speaks of heaven as a holy mountain where God's people live forever. (Isaiah 11:9, 56:7, 65:25)

Unfortunately, this beautiful picture was lost sight of as Israel began to emulate the pagan view of God. The temple moving to a mount began during Solomon's reign which makes sense because he was also the first King to commission building pagan high places throughout Israel. 1 Kings 11:7 tells us that "Solomon built a high place for Chemosh the abomination of Moab... and for Molech the abomination of the children of Ammon." After Solomon, the presence of high places persists throughout Israel like a cancer. Some kings get rid of them only for other kings to rebuild them. It was a constant back and forth until the worship of the true God-who-dwells-among-you was completely forgotten.

Social Injustice

It should come as no surprise then that just as Solomon moved away from a YWH cosmology, his social actions also reflected the ways of the fallen kingdoms. For example, did you know the temple Solomon built was dependent, not on the freewill offering of passionate worshipers, but on slave labour?

Hard to swallow right? In fact, I wouldn't believe it either if it weren't for the fact that the Bible itself tells us:

> Now King Solomon levied *forced laborers* from all Israel; and the *forced laborers* numbered 30,000 men... (1 Kings 5:13) [T]his is the account of the *forced labour* which King Solomon levied to build the house of the Lord... (1 Kings 9:15, *Italics supplied*)

Don't miss the contrast here: When God told Israel to build him a sanctuary, he invited all who were *willing* to bring offerings

(Exodus 25:1), and the people volunteered the funds, resources, and labour (Exodus 35:21-29). By contrast, Solomon's temple was built by heavy taxation and forced slave labour (1 Kings 5:13-16, 9:15).

To top it off, as we saw in the previous chapter, it was Solomon's taxes and slave labour—used to build the temple among other beautification projects—that caused the nation of Israel to splinter when his son Rehoboam took the throne. And once it splintered, it never recovered.

Shock Numero Dos

Despite all the above drama, God does something unexpected—he still blesses the new temple. The story tells us his presence filled it just as it filled the tent in the wilderness. God also referred to Solomon's temple as "my house" on multiple occasions, and in many other texts, God says he is glorified in this temple. In fact, Jesus himself is zealous for the temple during his earthly ministry and calls it, "my house." (Matthew: 21:12-14)

Isn't that odd? Why would God say he didn't want a permanent house, and then embrace one as though he always wanted it? Did he change his mind? Did the *bling* of Solomon's temple somehow win God over?

I think the answer to this seeming contradiction is really simple. Think back to the whole, "give us a king" chapter in 1 Samuel 8. God told Israel he didn't want them to have a king like the other nations, but they insisted, so he gave them a king and guess what? *He even blessed the king.* In fact, Jesus came from the lineage of the Davidic dynasty and God's blessing was clearly over this royal household. But that doesn't mean God changed his mind about the whole king thing. In the end, the whole "king thing" was disastrous for Israel. And it was the same with the Solomonic temple.

Here's the thing: God isn't ego driven. If the people insist on a permanent temple he doesn't want, he isn't going to spend the next 1000 years throwing a hissy fit. As in the "give us a king debacle," God worked with his people and did his best to turn a bad situation toward the best possible outcome.

God seems to be so full of grace, so devoid of ego, that even when we do what he doesn't want he finds a way to make it beautiful.

But it doesn't change the fact that this was never his desired will. And because it wasn't, Solomon's temple project set in motion a series of events that ended in Israel's splintering and eventual collapse. And in that defeat, as the armies of Babylon marched into Jerusalem, the Solomonic temple met its end, never to be seen again.

But that's not the shock...

Solomon's temple was gone. But this wasn't the end of the Temple story in Israel. Even as the Jews were led into captivity, God had already promised that in 70 years, they would return to their homeland and rebuild it. (Jeremiah 29:10) And it wasn't just his people he said this to. Cyrus, king of Persia, received visions from God that involved, not simply the return of the Jews to Jerusalem but even the rebuilding of the temple.

> Thus says Cyrus king of Persia, 'The Lord, the God of heaven... has appointed me to build Him a house

> in Jerusalem, which is in Judah. (2 Chronicles 36:23)

Kind of weird right?

I mean, a pagan king getting a vision about building God's temple? Sounds like this temple was a big deal for God—enough that he would ensure the most powerful human alive at the time was on board with the whole thing.

And true to form, when the Persians conquered Babylon, a decree was issued (by Cyrus) to restore and rebuild Jerusalem and its temple. (Ezra 1:1-4)

And the temple is rebuilt. (Yay!)

But that's not the shock either...

Here's the shock. The temple is rebuilt, but afterwards, something very odd happens. Or perhaps I should say, "doesn't happen."

Even though the prophets spoke highly of rebuilding the temple, and even though God himself used Cyrus as an instrument to rebuild what he referred to as his "house" for his "glory", something goes awfully wrong.

The presence of God, his "fire", his "Shekinah" glory, his cloud, his smoke (which filled the Tent and the Solomonic Temple) never, ever fill the second temple.

Now, I need you to appreciate how odd this is. God spoke highly of his temple. He said he wanted it rebuilt. He orchestrated its rebirth. He gave visions, instructions, and dreams. He spoke zealously of it as a place for himself and his majesty.

In fact, through the prophet Haggai, God said of the second temple:

> The glory of this latter temple shall be greater than the former,' says the Lord of hosts. 'And in this place I will give peace,' says the Lord of hosts. (Haggai 2:9)

And yet, when it's finally rebuilt... nothing.

God never shows up.[9]

His glory never fills it.

Shock Numero Tres

We have just seen Haggai's failed prophecy. The second temple wasn't more glorious than the first. Not only was it nowhere near as beautiful (Ezra 3:12), but the fire—the presence of God—never entered it.

So then, was Haggai wrong? Did he misunderstand God? Or did God himself get it wrong?

---

[9] The closest we ever come to God's presence manifesting in the Second Temple is in 2 Maccabees 3 and the story of Heliodorus, a Greek administrator to the king, who was ordered to take treasure from the Temple. God's supernatural power manifested and warded off Heliodorus and his men. However, this manifestation was temporary and not the same as the Shekinah glory we see in the original tabernacle.

Some have argued that Haggai's prophecy still came to pass because Jesus set foot in the second temple, and by doing so, the second temple became more glorious than the first.

However, this approach doesn't fully work. Haggai's prophecy is that the new temple will have:

A) more glory than the first, *and* that from it,
B) God would give peace.

But Jesus brought a complete and total end to the temple and its services. In other words, rather than an upgrade or elevation of the temple, the ministry of Jesus cancels it entirely.

The temple was also a constant centre of tension and controversy. Regardless of how one feels about the Apocrypha, one thing is clear—it is full of stories about the temple and the endless violence that surrounded it during the intertestamental period, including but not limited to Antiochus Epiphanes and his desecration of the temple. (1 Maccabees 1)

But the tensions don't end there. They continue into the NT. In fact, things got so bad that in AD 70, the Romans attacked Jerusalem and burned the temple to the ground. Doesn't sound like God was giving peace from this second temple at all.

So then, what on earth is going on?

It gets worse...

Before answering that question, I want to fast forward to our contemporary era. Today, many evangelical Christians await the arrival of what they refer to as a "third temple" which will be built in Jerusalem. This third temple, they believe, must be rebuilt in the same location as the first (Solomonic) and second (post-exilic) temples.

But there is a problem: The mountain is now occupied by another permanent sacred building—the Islamic shrine known as the "Dome of the Rock."

As you can imagine, Islamic-Jewish-Christian tensions have flared over this. In the 1990s, a plot to blow up the Dome of the Rock and spark an Israeli-Arab conflict was intercepted by authorities. But tensions continue. Some Christians believe that in time, the Dome will be destroyed allowing the third Temple to be rebuilt.

This kind of eschatological vision fuels xenophobia, Islamophobia, and Anti-Arab racism. These theological systems, in turn, influence American foreign policy via the conservative political right. And while this conflict is incredibly complex and multilayered, the consequences of this evangelical influence on middle east diplomacy have been constant war, bloodshed, and the deaths and displacement of thousands of Palestinians.[10] In fact, at the time of this writing, a new war has broken out in Israel/ Palestine resulting in thousands of deaths with no end or solution in sight.

The reasons for this conflict extend beyond temple tensions, but not apart from them. In wrestling with the question, "Why did Hamas and Islamic Jihad launch the attack?" an October 9, 2023, Guardian report titled, "Israel-Hamas war: what has happened and what has caused the conflict?" pointed to temple tensions as contributing to the violence.

---

[10] "Holy Land Christians feel abandoned by U.S. evangelicals," (Web: nbcnews.com)

> During the past week, some Jews have prayed inside the compound of al-Aqsa mosque in Jerusalem's Old City. The area around the mosque is known to Muslims as Haram al-Sharif and is the third holiest place for Islam after Mecca and Medina in Saudi Arabia. To Jews, it is known as Temple Mount, and is venerated as the site of the biblical Jewish temple. Jews are not permitted to pray inside al-Aqsa compound; to do so is highly provocative.[11]

Just like the pagan temples of old, just like Solomon's temple, and just like the second temple, social injustice is never far away from these permanent structures. And this is evidence enough that the will of God is not in harmony with these permanent temple projects. They are never what he wanted. They are never what he desired. Sure, he blessed and worked with fallen, sinful humans. But his actual plan was always in the background, and he acquiesced for a time but only to lead us back to what his heart has always desired.

Look at it this way: Remember how God never wanted Israel to have a king, but then he let them have a king anyhow? Follow the storyline. God went ahead and gave them a king and then he instructed the kings and blessed them—especially David. However, this isn't because God changed his mind about human kings but because through the selfish demands of fallen people, God was going to reaffirm his original plan. And as expected, the lineage of David brought Israel to Jesus.

---

[11] "Israel-Hamas war: what has happened and what has caused the conflict?" (Web: theguardian.com)

In other words, God worked through the human dynasty he never wanted to lead us back to the divine dynasty he always had in mind.

The temple project works the same way. God never wanted permanent temples. But he blessed them anyways because through them he would bring us back to what he always wanted. Through the Solomonic temple, and the post-exilic temple, God would lead us toward the true temple he always had in mind.

So, when Jesus comes to earth, he honours the temple, but ultimately, he brings it to an end. With his death and resurrection, Jesus births something new. A new kind of temple. A new kind of tabernacle. A new kind of embassy between heaven and earth. A temple whose glory far transcends the Solomonic and post-exilic structures. A temple filled with the Spirit of God. A temple that is mobile and simple, bringing the heart and peace of God right into the lives and homes of everyday people.

And you know what this temple is:

> Do you not know that you [the church] <u>are the temple of God</u> and that the Spirit of God dwells in you? — 1 Corinthians 3:16-17

> Now, therefore, you are no longer strangers and foreigners, but fellow citizens with the saints and members of <u>*the household of God*</u>, having been built on the foundation of the apostles and prophets, Jesus Christ Himself being the chief cornerstone, in whom the whole building, being fitted together, grows into a holy temple in the Lord, in whom you

> also are being built together for a dwelling place of God in the Spirit. — Ephesians 2:19-22
>
> *(Notice how in this verse, the "building" is not built with brick and wood, but with people.)*
>
> For... you [the church/ people] are God's building. — 1 Corinthians 3:9-11
>
> [Y]ou also, as living stones, are being built up a spiritual house, a holy priesthood, to offer up spiritual sacrifices acceptable to God through Jesus Christ. — 1 Peter 2:5
>
> And what agreement has the temple of God with idols? For you are the temple of the living God. As God has said: "I will dwell in them, And walk among them. I will be their God, And they shall be My people." — 2 Corinthians 6:16

There is a lot I can say about each of these texts, but for now I just want to point out one thing: *The NT church is nothing like the permanent temples.*

On the contrary, it is a return to the original wilderness tabernacle. Paul calls our bodies "earthly tents" (2 Corinthians 5:1), and like the OT Tent, these earthly tents are now the dwelling place of God's Spirit. This means God's new Temple is mobile again. It is also simple because rather than a building, it's all about hospitality and friendship. This new temple is also on level ground instead of a mountaintop, for as everyday people we live among others, in the neighbourhood and apartment buildings of our cities and towns. Social harmony and justice is central to the NT church, for in it we see a new civilization that moves to the rhythms of God's heart, and not the oppressive ways of empire.

In fact, Paul teaches that all the walls that divide us in fallen culture have been removed by Jesus. (Galatians 3:28) We are a new humanity, filled with the fire of God's presence, and this new church far from being beautiful on the outside (like the Taj Mahal, St. Peter's Cathedral, or the Mahabodhi) is made beautiful by one thing: *"Christ in you, the hope of glory."* (Col. 1:27)

Shock number 3 is this: The church is the true temple God always wanted, and it's patterned after the true temple just like the OT Tent was:

GOD'S TENT	THE CHURCH
A Tent	A Tent (of Human Bodies)
Mobile	Mobile
Simple	Simple
Situated on level ground, in the middle of camp	Lives where the people are, in the neighbourhood
Justice was Central	Justice is Central
Filled with God's Fire	Filled with God's Fire
Beauty on the Inside, Not Outside	Beauty on the Inside, Not Outside

Finally, after thousands of years of fancy-temple detours, God leads humanity back to his original plan. Because it was never about a building, never about a program, never about ceremonies or rituals, never about rules or external parade—it was always about community, always about connection, always about togetherness, withness, and oneness.

And now, finally, he births his secret plan of an authentic community, a new humanity, a new civilization that moves to the rhythms of relationship, not religion. That new thing, that secret, that great mystery hidden in his heart from the beginning of time is the church.

Shock Numero Quatro

But there is another shock waiting for us. To see it, we need to go back to Haggai's "failed prophecy."

The one where he said the second temple would be more glorious than the first and from it, God would give peace.

And then it never happened.

How do we make sense of this? It's actually super simple:

Set in the context of the rebuilding of the second temple, Haggai's prophecy might sound like it's all about the second temple. But a closer look shows that, in truth, it has nothing to do with the second temple. On the contrary, it's talking about something else entirely. Just read his vision with a bit more context:

> [T]hus says the Lord of hosts, 'Once more in a little while, I am going to shake the heavens and the earth, the sea also and the dry land. I will shake all the nations; and they will come with the wealth of all nations, and I will fill this

> house with glory,' says the Lord of hosts. 'The silver is Mine and the gold is Mine,' declares the Lord of hosts. 'The latter glory of this house will be greater than the former,' says the Lord of hosts, 'and in this place I will give peace,' declares the Lord of hosts." (Haggai 2:6-9)

Did you catch it? Read in its proper context, the vision of Haggai has nothing to do with the second temple. It's a vision about the end of time when the second temple is no more. So, phrases like "this house" and "this place" cannot possibly refer to the second temple. They must refer to the only earthly temple left at the second coming of Jesus—that is the church.

At the second coming of Jesus, God will shake the heavens and the earth, he will shake the nations and reclaim the wealth they have exploited and will fill his house with glory. And what is this house? It's the only house that remains when Jesus returns—not a permanent temple in Jerusalem, but a house of people, a community, a family. This house will be filled, and when it is filled a new civilization will begin—a kingdom of other-centred love. And from that house, God will give peace. And peace will fill the cosmos once more, never to depart again.

This family, this house through which God will accomplish this, is his church. Not a building. Not an institution. Not a denomination with a logo and tax file number. A family of people redeemed by Jesus—a new humanity that is filled with him; mini-temples, mobile, simple, beautiful, and full of his Spirit.

It is through them, through us, through this great mystery hidden in his heart from the beginning of time, that God will fill the earth with his glory.

Shock Numero Cinco

These shocks have been heavy. I get that. But this final one, oh boy. This one is the big one.

Some years ago, I chaired a business meeting at a fairly traditional SDA church I was pastoring in my city. And a large part of the agenda that evening revolved around a simple question: Should our church host an annual Christmas program when Christmas is pagan?

The discussion lasted almost the entire meeting.

And it took every ounce of discipline in my possession to maintain a cool composure.

But this isn't strange or even new. Churches have been complaining about pagan influences for a long time. Over the years, I have written and created content on this topic, so I don't want to go into all that here. Suffice to say, pagan-panic culture is something I am sure most readers of this book are familiar with.

The argument goes something like this:

The Bible says, "pagan bad." So, therefore, as faithful believers we must avoid any association with "pagan bad." If we let "pagan bad" into the church, we will sin. And sin bad too.

And here's the thing. People who argue this aren't entirely wrong. All throughout the OT, God instructs his people not to copy the ways of the pagans that surround them. And whenever the people do, problems always follow. As we saw at the start of this chapter, Solomon's temple-project reflected many of the pagan temple elements and, of course, we see how that turned out. So, I agree with traditionalists, conservatives, and fundamentalists when it comes to this.

However, there is a sense in which I disagree. But I think it will be easier to explain via a chart. So here goes:

Neutral Pagan Influence *Cosmetics*	**Negative Pagan Influence** *Cosmology*
Expressive and artistic elements used in worship and cultural life.	The story we tell of who God is, what he is like, and how to worship him.
Ex: Instruments for worship, altars, animal sacrifices, priesthoods, etc. Both Pagans and Israel did these, and God was not concerned with the similarities.	Pagan ideas of God were often coercive and cruel. Pagan methods for worshipping God created barriers between people and God. God unequivocally rejects these.

OK, let me explain the chart above a little bit and then we'll get onto the final shock you are patiently waiting for.

The first column refers to Pagan influences that are neutral. They are things God doesn't seem to care about. For example, when we read of Nebuchadnezzar's statue in Daniel 3, and the instruments used to worship it, we find that the same instruments are mentioned in the Psalms for the worship of YWH. There is a similarity there that God doesn't care about. Likewise, pagan cultures that surrounded Israel practised animal sacrifice—often with the same animals as Israel. They had priesthoods just like Israel. Sacred sites just like Israel. Altars just like Israel. And so on.

God never said to Israel, "don't use animals, use insects instead so that we don't look like the pagans." Likewise, he never told the Israelites, "The pagans use those same instruments, so get them out of here."

When it comes to these modes of human creativity and expression, God seriously doesn't seem to care how similar we are to pagans. These issues are merely cultural cosmetics. They are neither here, nor there.

Where God does draw the line is when his people adopt practices and systems that lead toward pagan cosmologies. A cosmology is different to a cosmetic. For example, in Daniel 3 the instruments used in worship, and the fact that worship takes place when the instruments play, and that people bow to the ground—are all things Israel did as well under God's instructions. None of this is bad just because pagans do the same things. But in Daniel 3, there is more than cosmetics at play. There is also cosmology. The statue represents Nebuchadnezzar's anti-God vision of an eternal Babylon, the entire worship gathering is forced, coercive, and tyrannical. The death penalty, enforced by civil power, bullies the masses into compliance. This worship of empire, grounded in coercion and enforced by threat is not a cosmetic, it is a cosmology.

Pagan cosmologies[12] at the time were rooted in very cruel pictures of a god or gods. These pictures formed the

---

[12] I want to be clear that when defining pagan cosmologies in this chapter I am only referring to the cultural context described in the Old Testament. This is not a blanket critique of all pagan cultures in history.

foundations for how society functioned. If your gods were cruel, the tendency to nurture a cruel society was higher. This is why social injustices always accompanied idol worship. Idols were more than just dumb statues. They were icons that represented a culture's view of divinity, and from them, a complex social and cultural code would evolve. These codes were often coercive and benefited the strength of empires and elites while exploiting the marginalised and vulnerable.

But most problematic to these cosmologies was the means through which one entered into partnership or relationship with the divine. The use of magic, sorcery, and orgies was intended to manipulate the spirit world, or gods, into providing humanity whatever it needed to get through the next season. Human sacrifices would often be reserved for extreme scenarios in which the group would find itself in a position of existential vulnerability or threat. The sacrifice would appease the angry god and they would relent from their punishment.

On the contrary, the God of Israel did not need to be manipulated. He provided everything his people needed. He even cared for the wicked. He forbade human sacrifices because the only sacrifice needed, he would offer in himself, through his own son. And relationship with him was based on relational covenants rooted in grace, compassion, and understanding.

So, while God never concerned himself with the cosmetic similarities between Israel and the pagan nations that surrounded them, he certainly did everything he could to prevent Israel from adopting the cosmological practices and systems of the pagans.

Even when they demanded a king and insisted on building a permanent temple, both pagan cosmological practices, God spoke to them and promised to bless them if they stuck close to his law and followed his way. In doing so, God was trying to steer them as far away from the pagan cosmologies as possible. But in the end, the cosmologies won, and Israel became more corrupt than the pagan nations that had once occupied the land of Canaan.

But why am I saying all this? Because today, when you go to church, you see a whole lot of pagan-panic that almost always revolves around cosmetics. People complain about music, instruments, dress styles, hairstyles, harmless Christmas decorations and so on.

But what I never hear these folk complaining about is the pagan cosmology already present in how we do church.

Again, God doesn't care too much about pagan cosmetics.[13] But cosmology he resists. Why? Because in many instances, pagan cosmology creates walls between people and God. It puts his temple on a mountaintop instead of a neighbourhood. It makes his presence static instead of mobile. It surrounds him in costly jewels and precious metals, instead of authentic friendship and

[13] There are times where pagan cosmology and cosmetics overlap so much that God does ask his people to detach from them. For example, jewellery designed to demonstrate allegiance to certain pagan gods, near eastern tattoo practices with immediate occultic significance (not secular), and even certain styles of beard grooming mentioned in the OT. Then, there are times where God takes no issue with similarities between Israel and its pagan neighbours, going so far as to employ the imagery himself (for example, the snake on the pole in Numbers. Mesopotamian myths utilised serpent gods frequently). The point always seems to come back to cosmology and the picture of God we are anchoring and orbiting in our communities. For a more thorough treatment on this topic, see "Ancient Near Eastern Thought and the Old Testament: Introducing the Conceptual World of the Hebrew Bible", by John H. Walton

compassion. It emphasizes external beauty instead of hospitality and connection. It cultivates hierarchical social structures and conventions that exploit the voiceless while enriching the elite. It fuels social injustice and disharmony, instead of healing and community.

And this is shock number five—the final shock that might prove to be the hardest of all to swallow. That we Adventists (myself included) often nurture communities and local church cultures that put us right in line with pagan cosmologies, even as we work hard to avoid pagan cosmetics.

How so?

We separate the church from the people until church becomes irrelevant. We treat the church like a sacred building and shame congregants into silence. Parents of small kids often cop the worst of this, with nasty stares and passive-aggressive comments. We have traditions and social codes that make it hard for people to reach God. We demand people climb a long mountain of behavioural and cultural standards to get to God. We enforce Eurocentric cultural demands that people must comply with in order to belong. We use language, music, and customs that are out of touch and off putting to new generations, and we present a God that needs to be appeased by perfect behaviours no one can achieve. We might not sacrifice our children on fire, but we sacrifice them on the altars of legalistic obsession and our blind worship of tradition.

And it's this system, this structure that dominates many of our local churches, that is the true paganism the Bible warns against. These churches fight tooth and nail to keep pagan cosmetics out of the church, but in the meantime, they don't realise that they are operating according to a pagan cosmology, complete with its angry picture of God, its social injustices, and the endless walls it builds between people and heaven.

Conversely, the church the NT envisions is like the OT tent. Churches that embrace this model might find that in their cosmetics (music, style, aesthetics), they look similar to the cultures around them—because seriously, who cares? For the most part, that stuff is neither here nor there.[14] But what makes these churches incredible, is that they are fully committed to the cosmology of Jesus. They are people-centred, relationship-focused, and authentic communities. They do life with the people and refuse to place any walls between people and God. They are passionate about justice and compassion, committed to hospitality and Christlikeness, and are filled with the Spirit of God. They resist the way of empire and the commodification and consumerism of the age. In a land of artificiality and loneliness, they are genuine, and they are community.

And it is through this kind of church—this new temple Jesus birthed—that the vision of Haggai will eventually become a reality. The glory of God will fill the earth, and peace will flow like a river.

---

[14] For a more thorough treatment on this topic, see "Deconstructing the Adventist Worship Wars" on thestorychurchproject.com.

CHAPTER 6

SHADOW

The narrative of the OT Tent is really heavy stuff. Not only is it heavy, but it can also be incredibly and frustratingly tedious and boring. Yep, I said it. This whole "sanctuary doctrine" business can be really, really boring. I mean, even the word "sanctuary doctrine" is enough to send most folk into hibernation.

In fact, in all my years as a pastor, I have never met anyone who gets pumped about the sanctuary unless they were a theological nerd of some sort. Outside of this small circle of tabernacle geeks, no one really finds the topic interesting or applicable to their faith or lived experience.

But the problem, I have found, isn't so much the topic itself. It's how we talk about it as a church.

I remember as a kid having lots of Bible studies on the sanctuary, and they were always the same. Our Sabbath School teacher would start off with an overview of the architecture and layout, then move into the symbols and furniture in each of the compartments, he would then spend an inordinate amount of time dissecting every nook and cranny of the "articles" in the tent, and finally, he would make theological applications—most of which were super scary. But thankfully, by that point the teacher had already lost me, so as he got full into all the stuff that causes religious trauma, I was off thinking about Ninja Turtles and pizza.

So, here is my promise to you. In this chapter, I want to talk a bit more about the sanctuary, especially its trans-terrestrial significance. But we are NOT going to do it in the old school, super nerdy way. No analysis of sanctuary architecture. No geeky breakdown of every symbol, no tedious dissecting of all the furniture, and definitely no legalistic, religio-centric applications that cause anxiety disorders.

Not going to happen.

Instead, I want to keep things simple, explore the narrative arc of sanctuary in scripture, and look at why it matters to us here, now, in real-time—especially as it applies to the theme of the NT church. And to make things even better, this chapter will be short, sweet, and no more than ten pages.

So Much We Don't Know

Let me begin by saying this. The sanctuary in scripture is a mystery. There is a lot we don't know. All we have are glimpses and snippets—enough to know something epic, transcendent, and radical is being communicated. But not enough to piece it all together.

The sanctuary theme in scripture seems to be a trans-dimensional phenomenon that is too "beyond" for our language to properly convey. It would be like a 2D character using 2D language to describe a 3D cube or sphere. His words—all constrained to the limitations of a flat plane—would never be capable of expressing the awe of 3-dimensional reality. Try as he might, he will always come up short.

OK, I admit, that was a bit nerdy. And that's as bad as it's going to get. My basic point is this, the Bible gives us brief glimpses at this sanctuary thing, but never enough to fully comprehend it. It's just too much for us. That's why it has so many symbols and art. It's an immersive and somatic attempt at getting humans to experience something that is beyond human and beyond our physical dimension.

What We Do Know

But here is what we do know—the sanctuary in scripture is an eternal theme, a story, not merely a structure Israel built.

And if we inhale the theme and inhabit the story, it all starts to make sense.

I've broken that story down into five subheadings. They are:

THE SANCTUARY

Is a Shadow

Centres on "Withness"

Celebrates Connection

Promises Restored Oneness

Upholds Cosmic Justice

Allow me to comment on each of these briefly.

Is a Shadow

The sanctuary in the Bible is more than a tent the Israelites built. It is a divine reality. Paul tells us that the terrestrial sanctuary was a "copy" and a "shadow" of a heavenly/ trans-terrestrial reality. (Hebrews 8:5)

There is a ton we don't know about this divine reality. And the terrestrial tent isn't exactly like the divine. But it captures the same story as the divine and transports it into the human experience. What this means is that in some sense that we can't fully grasp, the sanctuary is a thing that conveys God's heart.

To put it differently, God has a sanctuary heart. This isn't something that starts in Exodus. His heart has always been "sanctuary."

Centres on "Withness"

But what does that mean? When God told the Israelites to make him a sanctuary, he gave the reason behind it: "So that I may dwell among them." (Exodus 25:8) In fact, there is a beautiful verse found in the Apocrypha which says,

> You, Lord, who need nothing, made the temple your dwelling among us. — 2 Maccabees 14:35

This "dwelling among" or desire to be "*with*" is what I refer to as the "*withness*" of God. To put it in simpler terms, God's withness means he loves to be "with" people.

To enjoy someone's company goes beyond a mere declaration of love. After all, you can love someone and not want to be around them much. To enjoy someone's company, to want to live among them, implies that you don't just love the person, you like them. So, to borrow from David Asscherick, "God likes us." And this isn't a development in the story of scripture. Because the sanctuary is God's heart, and because it is a trans-terrestrial phenomenon (meaning the earthly tent was based on an eternal reality) this means that God's eternal posture toward us is that he not only loves us, *he likes us* and longs to be "with" us.

Celebrates Connection

Because God loves to be *with*, you can imagine the pain sin brought to his heart. Sin causes separation. And nothing could be worse for a God who made us to be "with" than to be separated from us eternally.

So, God activates his redemptive plan, a plan of reconciliation, in which God himself bridges the gap in order to restore the broken connection and bring us back into relational oneness with him.

In short, sin separates humanity from God, but the sanctuary tells an immersive story of how that connection is restored forever through his own self-sacrifice.

Promises Restored Oneness

This "forever" is defined by one central thing: *relational oneness*. No more separation. No more broken friendship. No more enmity. Through the gospel, God restores all things back to an ecosystem of relational oneness with himself.

This is why Ellen White says that in the end,

> One pulse of harmony and gladness beats through the vast creation. From Him who created all, flow life and light and gladness, throughout the realms of illimitable space. From the minutest atom to the greatest world, all things, animate and inanimate, in their unshadowed beauty and perfect joy, declare that God is love. — The Great Controversy, 677, 678.

That one pulse of harmony is a universe restored to relational oneness with God. This restoration is hinted at in the "Day of Atonement"—a central ceremony in the sanctuary system.

What does atonement mean? The simplest way to describe it is to take the word "Atone" and split it in two. You end up with "*At One*." Because that's what this day is all about. It is God's final cleansing act through which all things are brought back into that relational oneness.

Cosmic Justice

Once the Day of Atonement ended, the Israelites would have a "Feast of Tabernacles" which was basically a 7-day party that celebrated the abundance of God. This feast points forward to a new world and a new society in which ecological and social harmony are restored to the earth.

This demonstrates that smack at the heart of God's sanctuary heart lies a love for the marginalized, the oppressed, and the suffering—that is a heart of justice.

We see a strong link to this in the story of Jesus "cleansing" the temple of all the merchants in Matthew 21:12-17. Jesus disrupts the corrupt consumerism that has taken over the temple, but have you ever noticed the end of that story? Jesus didn't do this simply because he wanted a quiet temple that didn't tick God off with too much noise (as some fundamentalist reverence trolls would have us believe). The end of the story shows us why Jesus did this:

> And Jesus entered the temple and drove out all who sold and bought in the temple, and he overturned the tables of the money-changers and the seats of those who sold pigeons. He said to them, "It is written, 'My house shall be called a house of prayer,' but you make it a den of robbers." *And the blind and the lame came to him in the temple, and he healed them.* (Italics supplied)

Notice who came into the temple after Jesus cleansed it: *the blind and the lame*. That is the misfits, those who weren't allowed in before, those who didn't fit in, those who were ostracised and kept on the outskirts. Jesus cleanses the temple, not because he is a religiously obsessed prude, but because he has a heart for the marginalized.

This heart, this passion for justice and compassion, is at the very centre of the sanctuary. And in the end, the story of the sanctuary promises us a cosmic justice tribunal in which all the unjust systems, structures, cultural conventions and institutions will come crumbling down and a new world of abundance and inclusion will emerge.

Bringing it All Together

These 5 basic ideas are the bits that really matter about this whole sanctuary thing.

They tell the eternal story of the sanctuary and reveal God's eternal posture toward creation—a posture of divine neighbour. It's no surprise then that John 1:14 says, "the word became flesh and dwelt among us."

The Greek word translated "dwelt" literally means, "to pitch one's tent."

Jesus is God in human flesh, he is God in human-tent form. He is God's sanctuary heart revealed, not in a structure, but in a person.

So, of course, it's also no surprise when Jesus, speaking of his own body, said, "destroy this temple, but I will rebuild it in three days." (John 2:19)

Which means, it's should be no surprise that at the end of scripture, Revelation 22:3 tells us that "the tabernacle of God is *with* men, and He will dwell *with* them, and they shall be His people, and God Himself will be *with* them." (Italics supplied)

And finally, it should not shock us that John declares in Revelation 22:21, "I saw no temple in it [The New Jerusalem], for the Lord God the Almighty and the Lamb are its temple."

Honestly, unless you are a Levitical nerd, there's no need to go further. The story of the sanctuary is simple.

God wants to be with us.

Why it Matters

When the OT Tent was built, it was built in a way that reflected the heart of this sanctuary story. This is why the tent was simple, mobile, and at the centre of camp. The tent was a shadow of a higher reality. It told a story. A story of God's withness that was lost in the Solomonic and post-exilic temples but restored in Jesus and his church.

This is why Christ's new temple—his church—is not a building, a program, or an event—it is a gathering of people in a simple, dusty, near eastern home. And in being so, the new temple returns to the pattern of the first, which was patterned after the trans-terrestrial, which is itself a portal into God's eternal heart of love. The church in this sense is a shadow of something greater as well—a shadow of God's heart.

Sadly, today many local churches are engineered to do the opposite. They communicate a story, yes, but not the story of the sanctuary. Some churches boast impressive programming, next-level productions, and a fun factor that is enviable.

Others boast traditions and standards that they feel make them more acceptable to God. But in the end, both types of churches focus on what God never asked for while overlooking what he's always been about: *withness*. Rather than portals to his heart, they often become barriers without even knowing it.

I don't say this to be destructive or mean spirited. I say it because we all know it, and its time we wrestled with it honestly and humbly.

Authentic community is missing in almost all our local churches. Meaningful connection with our neighbourhoods and cities is practically non-existent. Legalism, perfectionism, and an endless obsession with rules occupy our attention. There is no passion for the marginalized, the oppressed, or the misfits. Many of our churches shut their eyes to real injustice in their communities but will go to war against silly, superficial things. We preach passionately about the sanctuary, geek out on its details, host long seminars on the stuff, but ignore its story and the practical application of that story in real-time.

And truth be told—it will always be this way. You and I are not going to fix all the problems of the church. But what we can do, what we should do, is search for the ways in which God is moving in our city and join him there. Because with or without us, God is going to do a new thing. We can choose, today, to be a part of what he is doing in the world. Of birthing new missional churches that function as shadows of the heavenly tent, which is itself a portal to God's eternal heart of love.

Just as the OT tent was a shadow of something greater, something radical and transcendent, so our churches can be shadows of the heart of God, providing hope, comfort, and connection to humanity and pointing everyone to something bigger and grander than ourselves—the heart of God, the trans-terrestrial mystery, revealed in earthly vessels.

CHAPTER 7

SPIRIT

One of the most common complaints that I hear among Adventists is, “we don’t have the Holy Spirit” or “we need the Holy Spirit.” Sermons on the “latter rain”—an end-of-time manifestation of the Spirit—are common in conservative evangelistic circles. Audio Verse has over 800 pages of Holy Spirit sermons ranging from topics like personal growth to mission and evangelism. In 2017, an entire Sabbath School quarterly was focused on the Holy Spirit. And Director of the NAD Evangelism Institute, Dr. Ron E. M. Clouzet even published a book titled, “Adventism’s Greatest Need: The Outpouring of the Holy Spirit.”

Among church members who long to see change in the church, prayers for the Holy Spirit are usually the first step. And if you listen to the “Holy Spirit conversations” during Sabbath lunch, you might hear phrases like “we need to pray that the Spirit is poured out” or, “we need to prepare ourselves to be filled by the Spirit.” You might even hear a few out-of-context Ellen White quotes about the Holy Spirit not showing up until we start being obedient to the 349,776,479 lifestyle standards we’ve come up with.

This kind of rhetoric might be toxic and discouraging, but to many it’s meant to serve as a logical explanation for why our local churches are not fulfilling their mission. If only we got our act together the Holy Spirit would come, and all our problems would go away.

The issue according to all this messaging is that the Holy Spirit is not here—at least not in a radical, supernatural, dramatic "Book of Acts" kind of way. The solution then is to do whatever it takes to get him to show up.

And here is where things get bizarre because, how do you summon the Holy Spirit? For some, it's all about "personal revival." For others, it's "reformation." Then there are the theology nerds in the church who think that if only everyone had a better grasp on doctrine, all our problems would be solved. So, bring on more cognitive driven Bible study programs. More doctrine-focused guest speakers. More events explaining Daniel and Revelation. And of course, there are those who think the key to getting the Holy Spirit to show up is stricter, more demanding moral commitments. So, bring on seminars on the health message, dress reform, and music styles. Because if we shame people enough, harass people enough, and coerce them into moral compliance then the Holy Spirit will come, right?

We would be mildly justified in assuming all these things if none of the above approaches had ever been tried before. But they have all been tried countless times. In fact, there are local churches that brand themselves based on one or more of the above approaches. But none of these methods have ever resulted in anything even remotely interesting. The Holy Spirit remains just as silent, and our local churches remain just as sleepy.

So then, do we need a new "summon the Holy Spirit" method? And if so, what is it?

The answer to the first question is yes and no. The answer to the second question is more complex. But in order to answer both, we need to go back to the story.

In the Beginning

The story begins in Genesis. The Bible tells us that the spirit of God was hovering over the chaotic waters. And then, God spoke, and creation began. The final step in his creative work was the birth of humanity.

I want you to notice something here because it's super important. Humanity came last in the creation story. But what was first? What initiated the whole thing? Where does the story begin? And the answer is simple. "In the beginning, God..." (Genesis 1:1)

In short, *God came first. Then man.*

But Moses gives us some extra context. Of the time before creation he says, "The earth was formless and empty. Darkness was on the surface of the deep..." (Genesis 1:2)

Sounds pretty bleak right? Formless. Empty. Darkness. Doesn't seem like the most promising scenario. If God was trying to bake a cosmic pie, these ingredients sure don't seem like the best options unless he was going for a mix of nihilistic flavours with a tinge of despair. But despite this bleak beginning, something appears in the story that moves everything in an unexpected direction. Moses adds, "and God's Spirit was hovering over the surface of the waters."

In the ancient world, waters represented chaos. You don't get anything useful from chaos, unless of course, there is an artist who specializes in repurposing chaos toward order and generating breathtaking beauty from the vacuous mix of formless and empty darkness. That artist is God, whose Spirit is there, hovering over the chaos with a clever idea—to take that churning mess of nothingness and terraform it into the only world you and I have ever known.

But this isn't a book about creation, so let me get to the point here. In this first story, we find a pattern in the biblical mind that will repeat over and over again. The pattern goes like this: *Spirit first, people second*.

Spirit First. People Second.

Fast forward to the post-Babel scenario and a man from an idolatrous family named Abram is called by God. God tells him that through Abram he is going to birth a new nation, a people that have not existed before. And that through these people, all other people on earth will be blessed. (Genesis 12: 1-3)

God is, of course, referring to the nation of Israel through whom the Messiah would come. But notice the pattern repeating itself here. Before the nation existed, before Abram even knew who YWH was, God had already planned it all out. In other words, the whole thing happened because God set it in motion. Had he not done so, Abram sure wouldn't have done it. The poor guy was off minding his own business, trying to figure out what to do after the Babel project collapsed. He had no intention of starting a new nation or lineage through whom a Messiah would come. But God did. Because this is the pattern throughout all redemption history: God first, people second.

This pattern repeats so often in the Bible that if I mentioned every instance, it would get overwhelmingly tedious. So, I'll only share a few more key ones before moving on.

God tells the nation of Israel to make him a sanctuary and then fills the tent with his Spirit. One might argue that the people had to build the sanctuary first, so this represents a "people first" scenario. But look deeper. First, God initiated the building of the sanctuary. Had he never mentioned it, no one else would have got the ball rolling. Second, and more important, however, is that the sanctuary God instructed them to build was a replica of the real thing that already existed in heaven that "the Lord pitched, not man." (Hebrews 8:2) So I rest my case: *Spirit first, people second.*

Then, of course, there is Jesus and salvation. Not only was it God's initiative, but the Bible goes so far as to say he planned it before the world even began. (Revelation 13:8) Why? Because *Spirit first, people second.*

People First, Spirit Second?

But the story isn't smooth. Things happen. Odd things. Strange things. Things that defy the pattern and go in the opposite direction. Things like Satan's "I will" rebellion (Isaiah 14:12-14 and Ezekiel 28) in heaven where he placed himself first, before God. Things like the fall of man where they went ahead of God and trusted in themselves instead of his heart. (Genesis 3) All these things reveal a counter-principle at work in the universe. One that reverses the pattern to a "people first, Spirit second" order.

In fact, it's more accurate to talk about this as the "all about me" counter-pattern, because once we place ourselves first, we tend to remove the Spirit from the equation altogether. He doesn't even come in second, third, or fourth. He just gets forgotten except for those few moments we might use him as a token to justify our actions.

A great example is a story we have already explored in detail: David and his temple project. David goes ahead of God and offers to build a temple God never asked for. Nathan the prophet mistakenly gives David the green light. But God intervenes and tells Nathan he needs to eat some humble pie and go tell David not to build the temple. Why? Because God already has a plan to build a temple. *Spirit first, people second.*

David appears to miss the point God is getting at, so he prepares Solomon to be the temple builder. (1 Chronicles 22 and 28) They move ahead of God, reversing the order of the pattern. And when it's done, chaos follows.

See that's the thing. The pattern in Genesis is that the Spirit takes chaos and brings order out of it and humanity is then invited to enjoy the beauty that emerges from that process. But when we reverse the pattern, we also reverse the process. We go from order backward into chaos. And this is precisely what happens with Solomon's temple project. And it's not his fault. In fact, it's not exactly David's fault either. David couldn't see the grand thing God was doing. It was hidden from him. And Solomon had been conditioned his whole life to believe he was the promised temple builder. David went as far as to say, "[God] said to me, 'Solomon, your son, shall build my house..." (1 Chronicles 28: 6) even though in the original message, delivered by Nathan, Solomon is never personally named. So, with the frailty of humanity in motion, Solomon goes ahead of God and does something God hasn't asked for. And in the end, despite God's gracious support, the economic and social injustice that it took to engineer this new temple split Israel in half, and the nation imploded.

But the story isn't over because none of this took God by surprise. As mentioned in a previous chapter, some might argue that Nathan's prophecy was meant to have a dual-application to both Solomon and Jesus. Solomon represents a fallen human attempt at building the temple in a human way. This would in turn serve as a contrast to Jesus as the original plan God always had in mind. Although I'm more inclined to argue the prophecy had nothing to do with Solomon, I do think there is plenty of room for these two interpretations. The main point still stands either way: Solomon and his temple project were never God's ultimate, his plan A, or his overall plan to begin with. The plan was always Jesus. The temple was always people. So, Jesus comes and dies on the cross. He was the lamb slain from the foundation of the world because, of course, *Spirit first, people second*. He came to reset the pattern. And what happens next is insane.

The God who Sits

After Jesus' resurrection, he told his disciples to wait for him in Jerusalem as he went back to heaven. The disciples did just as he asked and waited for the outpouring of the Spirit before launching into their mission (there's the pattern again). But did you ever wonder what Jesus did when he got up there? It's actually pretty cool.

The Bible tells us that after Jesus' ascension,

1. He went straight to the Father (Daniel 7:13),
2. To appear on our behalf (Hebrews 9:24)
3. Where he serves as our defender and helper (Romans 8:34)
4. He is crowned King and receives the Spirit (Acts 2:33)
5. And finally, he "sat" (Hebrews 1:3, 12:2)

Study the sanctuary day and night and you'll notice, the priest never sat. In fact, he didn't even have a chair. The only place where sitting was hinted at in the sanctuary was on the mercy seat which represented the throne of God. Jesus is the sacrifice. He is also the priest. But he is also the one who sits.

The significance of this can't be overemphasized. It speaks to his authority, his equality with the Father, his divinity and kingship and so many other themes. But two themes hit me hardest.

First, that Jesus is sitting because his sacrifice is complete and has been accepted. It's kind of like when the high priest was anointed in the OT (Exodus 29, Leviticus 8 and 21). At the anointing, oil was poured on the priest's head. According to Psalms 133, this wasn't just a smidge of oil like our modern thumb-to-forehead thing, this was a jar being poured until it ran down the face and beard of the priest, spilling on the ground beneath him. A similar scenario took place during the coronation of Israelite kings (1 Samuel 10:1), where oil was poured on the king to affirm his kingship over the nation.

This imagery helps us understand what's going on in heaven. Jesus returns to heaven and when he arrives, three significant things happen.

A. His sacrifice is accepted as perfect and complete. He is now the true high priest for all time.
B. Because he overcame, he is exalted above all others and crowned King of kings and Lord or lords.

C. Jesus "receives the Spirit" (Acts 2:33) anointing him as Priest-King.[15]

Jesus is now the Priest-King. As in the OT, this new Priest and King is then "anointed." But notice this: Anointings were always messy. Oil poured from the head to the ground. And just like the oil overflowed onto the ground of the OT priests and kings, so as Christ is crowned and anointed, the Spirit is poured on him and spills over. And as it spills over, a room full of disciples in Jerusalem receives the overflow of what has just happened in heaven. The anointing of the Spirit upon Jesus spills over and lands on them.

Peter said it best,

> Being therefore *exalted* by the right hand of God, and having *received* from the Father the promise of the Holy Spirit, he has *poured* out this, which you now see and hear. (Acts 2:33, italics supplied)

Don't miss those key words. Jesus "poured out" the Spirit, not because humans did something amazing but because he "received" the Spirit. And he "received" the Spirit because he

---

[15] The dynamic between Jesus and the Spirit is very mosaic. He was conceived by the Spirit (Mat. 1:20), filled and anointed by the Spirit (Luke 3:22, Acts 10:38), ministered in the Spirit (Luke 4:18), and offered himself through the Spirit (Hebrews 9:14). And yet, Acts 2:33 tells us something else happened between Jesus and the Spirit that hadn't happened before. Although the language is vague, it appears Jesus received the Spirit in a different, or perhaps fuller sense, (though the term "fuller" is arguable) at his coronation, and from that new receiving he poured it out on his people in a way never before seen.

was “exalted” by the Father. And he was “exalted” by the Father because his work of redemption was complete.

Wow.

Second, Jesus is sitting because the sacrificial aspect of his role has come to an end. He is the one sacrifice for all time. (Hebrews 10:14) As the redemption story moves on, someone else is now entering the picture. Someone humanity has only ever had glimpses of. Someone our species has never fully or truly experienced. Jesus sits because the time has come for the Spirit to enter the scene and do something that has never happened before. He is being poured out to fill this new temple of people and homes. If Jesus was act 1 of a redemptive play, the Spirit is act 2.

It’s kind of like a tag team in a wrestling match. One of the wrestlers does his work, then he tags his mate in and steps out the ring. Jesus sitting is like Jesus tagging the Holy Spirit: “*Your turn.*”

And just as promised, the Holy Spirit was poured out. But notice this: When the Holy Spirit appeared, the disciples did not have a perfect theology, no well-designed events, no international guest speakers, no travelling pastor celebrities, no fancy buildings with $30,000 dollar organs and pews, no bookstores stocked with devotionals and commentaries, no conservative cultural codes like ties, suits, pews or lecterns, no super cool bands or marketable pastors, and no bank accounts or retirement plans.

And yet the Spirit was poured out.

Why? Because the Spirit being poured out wasn’t about the believers and how good they were, it was about Jesus and his perfect work. Jesus finished the work of salvation. Jesus made an end of sin. Jesus birthed a new humanity. Jesus is the lamb slain from the foundation of the world. With his sacrifice complete, he is enthroned and anointed—not with a jar of olive oil—but with the Spirit itself. (Acts 2:33) And the Spirit is poured on Jesus in such overwhelming volume, that it overflows from his celestial throne down the tunnels and corridors of multi-dimensional space and time until at last, it crashes like fire upon a room full of simple first-century believers.

And here is my main point. The Spirit is poured out because of what Jesus has done. His work is complete. He is sitting. The Father accepts the sacrifice of the son, and just as the oil was poured out over the anointed priest and kings until it spilled on the ground, so the Spirit that Jesus received at his coronation spills over to his people. This means, you don't have to be perfect, do better, master all your convictions and become a nerdy theologian in order for the Spirit to be poured out. It's never worked that way. The Spirit comes because of Jesus, not because of us.

And do you know why?

Say it with me now: Because *Spirit first, people second.*

He's Already Here

What does this mean for us if we take this pattern seriously? It's really quite simple: it means that right now, as you read this book, as you wonder what to do about your struggling church, as you engineer plans and strategies to move forward, the Spirit is already up to something. He's already in motion regardless of your theological ignorance and imperfections. He doesn't depend on us to get it right. He's not twiddling his cosmic thumbs waiting for you to stop eating chicken, or to become proficient at the 2300 days, or to achieve moral perfection before he acts.

Pastor Mike Cyprian Manea makes the excellent point that such a man-centred theology—common in many conservative SDA churches—makes humanity a type of co-redeemer with God. It's a fundamentalist SDA version of Catholicism's Virgin Mary or pantheon of Saints whose merits and intercessions are needed to secure salvation. Only in our version, it's our behaviour and commitments that are needed for God to finally show up and do something on the earth. And until we get our act together, he just won't. But the gospel says the opposite. God is not waiting. He's not restrained. He's not restricted. He weaves his redemptive plan through our failures and in the end, he wins through us, with us, and alongside us—but never because of us.

One More Thing

Jesus is sitting. That's the premise of this entire chapter. But it doesn't end there. The Bible goes even further by suggesting something even more radical. Notice how Paul words it in Ephesians:

> But God, being rich in mercy, for his great love with which he loved us, even when we were dead through our trespasses, made us alive together with Christ—by grace you have been saved— and raised us up with him, and *made us to sit with him* in the heavenly places in Christ Jesus, that in the ages to come he might show the exceeding riches of his grace in kindness toward us in Christ Jesus. (Ephesians 2:4-7, *emphasis added*)

Did you catch that? The Bible teaches that not only is Jesus "sitting" but that we, the believers, are "sitting" with him.

Once again, this one simple idea is nested with tons of theological weight. But from the missional side of things, it means this: If we are sitting with Jesus, it's because we are resting in his finished work. What this means is, believers ought to live with a posture of spiritual rest. The work is finished. Therefore, anything we do must come from a place of rest. And this includes mission.

In other words, we must engage the difficult work of discipleship and the mission of spreading the gospel from a place of heart-rest. We must serve while "sitting."

Unfortunately, this is not what spreading the gospel looks like in most of our lives. For some, outreach, evangelism, and discipleship are exhausting endeavours that revolve around complex programming that is unsustainable. For others, mission takes the shape of friendship, which is great, but is often driven by feelings of guilt, shame, and toxic missiology. We are not trusting in the Spirit, relying on Jesus, or serving from a place of rest. Instead, we are trusting in ourselves by believing the lie that we are the hero of the story, that people's salvation depends on us, and that if we don't aggressively spread the gospel, the blood of the lost will be on our hands.

I'm sorry, but this is utterly false. Why? Because the Holy Spirit depends on no man. Because if we did nothing, donkeys and rocks would do it for us. Because the truth is, God doesn't need us. He wants us. And because he wants us, he calls us into co-creation with him. Sharing the gospel is an adventure we are invited into so that we can share in the awe and joy of being in partnership with God. It is not a task that depends on us. And what this means is, that as we serve with Jesus we can also serve like Jesus: *while sitting*.

Serving from a place of rest and stillness.

Because Jesus is sitting.

And we are sitting with him.

Why it Matters

There are two incredibly important reasons why this matters. First, because all this “do x-y-z” and the Spirit will come is straight-up false. The gospel isn’t about what we do. It’s about what God has done and is doing. Which means that right now, he is already up to something. With or without us, he is on the move.

Did you miss that? Let me make sure you didn’t. I'll say it again, in a different way:

The Spirit is already here.

Second, because any theology that insists, we can do something to make the Holy Spirit show up is a pagan theology. You and I don't summon him. And anytime humans try to force God's hand, chaos always follows. (Judas anyone?)

What this means is, the outpouring of the Spirit isn't something that happens because people did something to convince God. That view of the Spirit, the idea that our behaviour and actions can somehow activate or summon him, is essentially what magic, sorcery, and even temple prostitution were all about. Through spells and incantations, many near-eastern pagan religions aimed to manipulate or appropriate the power of the spirit world in order to bring about some needed result in the physical realm. Through worship orgies, these societies aimed to influence the gods into fertilizing the land so that the crops would grow. This perspective is based on a cosmology that sees the spirit world or the gods as indifferent or detached from us. If we want their help, we have to do something to trigger it. Humans, in this worldview, are the catalysts of history and survival. If the gods or spirits did anything, it's because humans found a way (magic, orgies, human sacrifice) to force them to act.

However, the Hebrew scriptures move in the opposite direction. You don't need to manipulate God or trigger him to action. Instead, God is the one who initiates and gets us moving. The basic idea then, is churches that thinks their theology, actions, or moral commitments are the catalysts for an outpouring of the Spirit are operating under a pagan view of God, not a biblical one. We don't move him. He moves us. As SDA pastor Rodolfo Avir put it, "The coming of the Holy Spirit has nothing to do with humans performing x or y. It is the doing of Jesus in Heaven."[16]

The Human Element

Now that we have that out of the way, we can wrestle with the following question: Isn't there something for us to do? I mean, Jesus did expect obedience from his disciples, not docile passivity. And isn't it true that the Bible calls us to be active agents in the work of God? And doesn't Ellen White say that the Spirit won't come if we just sit around and wait for it? And didn't the apostles work super hard, often tirelessly, putting their own bodies on the line in order to share the gospel?

---

[16] Avir, Radolfo. Facebook comment. February 11, 2023.

The answer to all the above is, *yes*. This chapter isn't saying "do nothing, just chill, she'll be right, Spirit will come when it comes." Not at all. The purpose of this chapter is to show that the Spirit is already up to something. We don't activate him. *He activates us*. And because he's already in motion, our task is to align ourselves with what he is already doing.

That word alignment is super important. Alignment is intentional. Alignment is about co-creating with Spirit, a companionship, partnership, collaboration, and joint venture. Because even though it's "Spirit first, people second", there are still two characters in that formula—Spirit and people—and both matter. However, the Spirit is already here. The work is already happening. Our task isn't to find some trick to get the Spirit to appear but to identify where he is already working and get on board.

Because here's the honest truth you guys—the Spirit is going to do what he's going to do with or without us. We can either participate with what he is up to, or we can sit on the sidelines holding prayer meetings asking for him to show up.

Enough of that.

Enough of begging for that which God has already promised to give us abundantly. Enough of searching for that which is already here. Enough of the wild theories (most of which end up being spiritually abusive) on why the Spirit isn't here and how we can get him to show up. It's time we opened our eyes and realized; he is already up to something grand in the world. He is already moving radically through our culture, our cities, our neighbourhoods and our art. He isn't sitting around waiting for SDAs to get it right before he moves. We're not that important.

Jesus was clear that if his people don't shout his praises, the work of the Spirit will not stop. Instead, his activity is so radical and so ever-present that if the people do not praise, the overwhelming dynamite power of the Spirit would spill over into inanimate stones and make them sing. (Luke 19:28-44) He isn't bound to us or by us. He is doing his thing. We can either get aligned and participate, or we can miss it altogether.

Why aren't we aligned?

The concept of aligning with where the Spirit is working might seem simple, but it raises lots of questions. For starters, why isn't it happening? Why aren't people engaged in what the Spirit is doing? Others might ask—Aren't we already doing this? We are following the blueprint, doing everything we're supposed to be doing, and the church is still struggling. What else is missing?

It's usually at this juncture that many well-meaning church-folk start to offer simplistic solutions.

"We need people to come to the prayer meeting." But they don't.

"We need to start a small group ministry." But it never lasts.

"We need to bring this guest speaker over to get us in shape." But the speaker comes and goes, and everything stays the same.

"We need to change the worship style." But the youth remain disengaged.

"We need to go back to singing hymns only." And the youth disengage more.

"We need to get a new Bible study group going where we can learn all about the sanctuary and the 2300 days and end time events." And when the study group is all said and done, no one knows what to do next and so everyone just goes back to doing nothing.

"We need to watch this YouTube link, read this book, attend this seminar, adopt this model." And the results, if any, are short-lived.

"We need to do more evangelism." And running the event wears your best talent out so much no one wants to do evangelism for the next 5 years.

Why does this keep happening? Why doesn't anything change?

The Region Beta Paradox

During an episode of *The Joe Rogan Experience*, British podcaster Chris Williamson explained a phenomenon that I believe can help us make sense of why our churches struggle so bad year after year. It's called the region beta paradox. Chris explains it this way:

> [I]f you only decide to act after you cross a certain threshold of 'badness' you can end up being stuck in region beta. For instance, the friend that should leave his job—really, really needs to leave his job—but it's just about passable. His boss isn't that much of a **** [and] maybe the benefits are OK. [Or] the person that stays in an apartment that's got some mould in

> the ceiling. It's not too much mould or whatever.
>
> All of these people would be better off if the situations were worse because it would galvanize them into actually doing something. You can get stuck in this chasm of comfortable complacency that sits somewhere in the middle. If things are good, great. No problem. If things are bad, great. Activate energy to go and make them good. [But] if things are just about passable, you end up being comfortably numb.

Comfortably numb.

Let that image sink in. Because that's essentially what Laodicea is. It's a church that is trapped in the region beta paradox. It thinks it's doing great but is actually stuck in a "chasm of comfortable complacency." Things would actually be better for Laodicea if they were really, really bad because maybe then, the church would spring to action. But because things are just about passable, the church does nothing.

I think the example of the frog in a boiling pot is a good one. Now, I don't know if it's true, but the story goes that if you put a frog in a pot of boiling water it will leap out instantly. If you put it in a pot of cool water, however, and then slowly boil it, the frog won't move. It will just sit in the pot until it's dead. It would have been better for the frog if the water was boiling because his instincts would have ensured his survival. But because it was comfortable, the slow boil killed it without it noticing. That's the region beta paradox—that you would be better off in a worse situation because oftentimes a better situation would actually be worse than the worse situation. (Dizzy yet?)

But how does this help us make sense of the condition of our churches?

The answer is simple, but warning—it's pretty intense.

The region beta paradox is alive in our churches, but what causes it? Our system (the way our local churches are structured) causes it, that's what.

Let me put it this way. If your city has 10 churches and 9 of them are on fire but 1 of them is struggling, you are justified in assuming that something is wrong with the members of the struggling church. They need revival. After all, every other church is on fire except them. So, the most natural trajectory would be to address the individual members and light a fire under them for mission.

But what do you do when every church in the city is struggling to stay alive, and not just the one? In fact, what do you do when the struggling-church-syndrome is happening all over the globe?

At this point, you can no longer assume the members just need revival.

At this point, you must be willing to consider that maybe, just maybe, we have a systemic problem on our hands, and not just an individual one.

Something is feeding this condition. Something is fuelling it. Something is perpetuating it across cities, states, cultures and countries. Something in our system is literally putting people to sleep.

It's time we stopped shaming our church members by insisting the church would come alive if only they got their act together, committed more, sacrificed more, and prayed more. The people are not the main problem. The system is.

Why? Because it's our system that keeps us in a region beta paradox state. The church is barely alive and desperately needs revival. But the lights will still turn on this weekend. The deacon will still unlock the building. The program will still tick along as usual. And who knows, you might even get a nice sermon. Nothing grand or life-changing of course. But it's "just about passable."

Mission and retention are suffering terribly. But guess what? The Sabbath School will still meet. Even if no one reads the lesson, we can just read each one right there on the spot. We'll start with Saturday, then read Sunday, then Monday all the way to Friday. By then, it's time to wrap up. Did anything incredible happen? No. But nothing horrible happened either. It was "just about passable," and that's enough.

We aren't reaching our community. Neighbours don't know who we are. But guess what? A few families in the church had kids turn 11 and are now preparing them for baptism. A guy who stopped attending years ago trickled back in and wants to do a profession of faith. And a few new families joined the church this year. Yes, they were already Adventist back in their home countries so technically, the church didn't "grow." But who cares? It's enough to make it look like something is happening even though the truth is, nothing of any note is really taking place. But that doesn't matter, does it? So long as our baptism rates are "just about passable," we can keep ticking along on life support.

The Holy Spirit isn't present. Our church life is monotonous. Relationships are cold. Community engagement is non-existent. It's clear the Spirit of God isn't here in any meaningful way, but guess what? We have a church manual, and so long as we follow it and tick the boxes, we will hobble along OK. We'll still have board meetings, business meetings, selection and nominating committees, and departmental events. Nothing remarkable will take place of course, but that's quite alright. The manual ensures that no matter what, you can always count on things being "just about passable."

And what feeds this state of comfortable numbness? Is it bad people? Is it lazy people? Is it uncommitted people?

Hardly.

Many of our members are hard workers. They hustle all week long. Some of them work in mines and on rooftops, in the dead of heat, building and engineering and creating incredible things. Some are farmers who feed the nation, up before the sun rises and down long after it sets. Others work for multi-billion-dollar corporations. They handle accounts worth millions. They lead teams and meet KPIs with impressive alacrity. Others are academics, medical professionals, law enforcement, military, and hospitality staff—all careers that require top-level professionalism, high emotional intelligence, and wild levels of bravery. Then there are the retirees with decades of wisdom and experience and a wave of new generations with enthusiasm and creativity ready to step into the world to make massive, long-lasting impacts in the career sectors they choose.

The psychologist Jordan Peterson expressed a similar sentiment when he said:

> You look around the city here and you see all these buildings go up. These men, they are doing impossible things. They're under the streets working on the sewers, they're up on the powerlines in the storms, in the rain. They're keeping this impossible infrastructure functioning. This thing that works in a miraculous manner. They work themselves to death, and often literally. ...there's a massive infrastructure of unbelievably hard working, solidly labouring, working class men breaking themselves in half on a regular basis making sure that everything that always breaks, works.[1]

Peterson is right. And church, guess what? Many of those people doing these impossible things—both men and women—are sitting in the pews of your local Seventh-day Adventist congregation every weekend. And they are wildly, unbelievably amazing.

So sorry, I just don't buy it. The problem isn't the people—at least, not exclusively or even primarily. They don't need more sermons on how to get on fire. They already have fire. It's present all week long at work, sport, and school.

So then, why isn't it transferring to church?

I believe the answer is simple, but oh-so painful. I derive no pleasure from writing these words. But sometimes, love demands honesty.

And after two decades of ministry in our church (volunteer and employed), I have to be honest, our local church system is a system that rewards passivity, maintains docility, and douses out the fire already present in the lives of our members.

It's a system that resists innovation, rejects creativity, and has no room for anyone who isn't a preacher or a musician. Everyone else—except maybe the AV guys and the admin folk whose entire ministry is church-centric and non-missional—literally just shows up and sits around, never using their gifts, their talents, their interests or their fire to light the world.

To make matters worse, the church doesn't really suffer from sidelining over half its talent. Why? Because we have a system that guarantees that no matter how disengaged, how lethargic, and idle and detached we remain, the show will still go on, complete with our favourite hymns and a sermon to boot. A system designed around spectatorship, where success is measured by attendance not discipleship, and where week after week the only thing the system requires of you is to show up, sit down, and enjoy the program.

Sound harsh? It is. Hyperbolic? Arguably. I am a Jersey-boy with Puerto Rican blood. We tend to be a bit extra on the best of days, so forgive my words if they were unnecessarily intense. I tried hard to communicate this with as much clarity and humility as possible, but chances are I didn't fare so well. If that's the case, read me with a grain of salt. My intention is to build, not tear down.

Here's what I am trying to say: We have to stop blaming the people for problems caused by a system. We have blamed the people enough and gotten nowhere. If the Spirit is not manifesting among us, maybe it's time we took a look at how our local churches are structured. Maybe it's time we explored the possibility that our churches are struggling because they actually inhibit people's spirituality. And the thing doing the inhibiting isn't unspiritual members, it's the system itself, the matrix under which we all operate. A program in a building with a bulletin that is engineered to sedate us at worst and give us nothing more than a weekly booster shot at best. A "wineskin" or "container" literally incapable of channelling the raw, radical power the Spirit has in mind for his people.

New Wineskins

Jesus said you cannot take new wine and put it in old wineskins. (Mark 2:22) The old wineskins cannot handle the acidity of the new wine. They will literally burst. And I wonder, can our old wineskins (conventional local church structure) handle a fresh outpouring of the Spirit? Or would the Spirit burst our system from the inside out?

The truth is, we don't need to do anything special to get the Spirit to show up because the Spirit is already here, in the neighbourhood, the homes, the streets and alleys, the clubs and pubs. The Spirit is weaving his redemptive plan through the networks of our city, tugging hearts, giving dreams, whispering invitations and calling his children home. He's here, church. And he is on the move.

So then, I return to the questions at the start of this chapter. Do we need a new "summon the Holy Spirit" method? And if so, what is it?

The answer is no. But there is still something we must do. To be precise, it's got less to do with "doing" and more to do with "*undoing*." To be aligned with the already-present Spirit calls us to *undo* the structures, systems, traditions and conventions that might have served us well in the past, but that today constitute an old wineskin incapable of receiving the new thing God is doing.

Therefore, to align means to discard the chains of tradition, break the shackles of religiosity, and swing open the gates of our comfortable and predictable spectator model that keeps the Spirit out. The sooner we liberate our talent, energy, and passion from programs to partnering with what God is already doing in our city, the sooner we will see the wave of fire that has been there all along. No longer restrained by the time-consuming execution of a repetitive weekend event, we will, at last, be free to partner with Jesus.

So, let's align with him. And if that means discarding things that keep us from aligning then so be it. Nothing matters more than co-creating with the Spirit and joining him in his redemptive mission for our cities and friends. The Spirit is already here. Away with the old wineskins. It's time for the new.

CHAPTER 8

IDENTITY

Imagine walking into a church gathering in the early decades of its existence. When you arrive, you notice a handful of differences from the church you attend each Sabbath. For starters, there isn't a greeting team. Instead, you are greeted by everyone. The other weird thing is you aren't in a special building. You are at someone's house in a regular old neighbourhood. Kids are running around gleefully, a few folks are in the kitchen preparing a meal, others are chatting by the entrance and others scattered about in various places. No one has special "extra holy" clothes on either. Everyone looks, well, normal.

In time, the group (roughly 20 people) gathers around the table to eat, share about God, pray, discuss scripture, and celebrate communion. There are no rows of chairs or pews, no lectern from which a sermon will be delivered, and no platform where the "program" takes place. In fact, much to your surprise, there is no program at all.

Instead, the entire meeting is very organic, unscripted, and deeply spiritual. Everyone participates together, even the kids. There is singing, praying, scripture reading and discussion like our churches today, but no dry formalities. And most interesting is how everyone keeps talking about the different plans they have for building the kingdom of God during the week. Some are involved in feeding the poor, others taking care of widows and orphans, and some even collecting discarded babies left out on the streets and taking them in to love and raise them.

They talk about ways to pool resources together to continue blessing others. But their motivation isn't to just be nice. Before the gathering concludes one thing is clear—these folk see themselves as citizens of a new civilization, the Kingdom of Heaven, and they long to manifest the way of that Kingdom in the here and now. Along the darkened avenues of Rome, they shine a light—not via tracts, flyers, or seminar advertisements, but through the power of lives lived in harmony with Jesus.
And despite all the other obvious differences between this early church and the one you attend each Sabbath, it's this daily Kingdom rhythm that stands out as the biggest difference to you. Church, for these early believers, isn't a "Sabbath" only activity. Instead, their entire lives appear to revolve around being the church every day and everywhere they go. For them, church is an identity, not an event.

Which brings me to my next "church is not":

Church is NOT an event that we attend.

The belief that "church" is an "event" we attend isn't something you will ever hear preached or taught in any of our sermons or Bible study guides. However, beliefs are most clearly articulated—not with theological statements—but with actions. And our actions as a church reveal that for most of us, church is not an identity that reshapes our entire being. It is an event we attend and a box we tick.

Don't believe me? Here are some clear examples:

- We constantly talk about "going" to church—a phrase that would have been entirely foreign to early believers. For the NT, church is not something you "go" to. It is a new *identity*.
- We constantly talk about how young people are "leaving church." And we measure success by how many people are "attending" church. If attendance is high, the church is successful. If it's low, the church is not successful. If our young people are in the building, they are doing good. If they are not, we are losing them. Never mind what the rest of the week looks like—everything revolves around being at the weekend event.
- We constantly ask, "how was church?" The "was" betrays our perception that church happened "back then, at that time and in that place." This idea is entirely foreign to the NT. Church isn't a compartmentalized something that "happened" last Sabbath. It is a new way of being that reshapes my entire being along all of time and space.
- We say super bizarre things that would have made no sense to an early Christian like, "I wasn't fed at church this weekend" or, "church doesn't meet my needs" or, "I like my church because it has a special kids program" or, "The worship band at our church is so much better" or, "I attend this church because it sings hymns and doesn't use a projector." If we said any of these phrases to an NT believer, they would have been entirely bewildered.
- We constantly talk about getting our unchurched neighbours to attend church. Getting them in those doors is the primal objective of most evangelistic local churches.

Here is another one that really irks me. What do we often say when someone has stopped attending church after having been hurt or offended by another member?

"You shouldn't stop attending church because someone hurt you. We don't go to church for people. We go for God."

This line irks me because the biblical word for church (*ekklesia*) literally means "group of people." So, when we say "we don't go to church for people, we go for God" what we are saying is "we don't go to the group of people for the group of people" which makes absolutely no sense. I can meet God anywhere and anytime. If I gather with the "group of people" it's because I want to fellowship with the "group of people."

The truth is this line often serves as a way to maintain the status quo of toxic church environments by spiritualising away the hard work of healing broken relationships. And nested within this oft-repeated phrase is tangible evidence that we see church as something to "go" to (an event where we meet with God) and not as a new identity that reauthors our entire existence (including our frayed and fragmented interpersonal relationships).

Allow me to use some basic illustrations to make this clearer. When I was in my early 20s, I joined the Army. Now the thing about being a soldier in the Army is that it's not a job and way more than a career. It's an identity. Once you put that uniform on, you become a new person. Everything about you must realign with this new identity. It would be unfathomable for a soldier to ask another soldier—how was Army last week? As if "Army" were some event we attended at prescribed times. Army is not a thing out there; it is who we are.

Francis Chan uses another example. He had a church member who used to belong to a gang. When he was in the gang life, everything he did revolved around being in the gang. It would have been completely unthinkable for one gangster to ask another gangster, "How was gang last week?" Why? Because gang life is not an event, it is a way of being that reshapes every part of a gang member's life.

The church is meant to be understood this way—as a way of life that reshapes everything, not an event we attend.

What the Church Is

In order to fully appreciate this, we need to go back to the story of scripture. And by back, I mean way back to the beginning.

According to Genesis, God's original design for humanity was a partnership with him in creating a beautiful world. Humanity was meant to work together in unison with God and one another to architect a world of beauty and connection. Had God's plan flourished without interruption, the earth would have been a global village without injustice, inequity, or disharmony.

But through rebellion, man separated themselves from God and each other. The post-Edenic world was a world—not of partnership and harmony—but of power struggles and social scaffolds designed to prop up the elite and exploit the masses. Men took whatever women they wanted as their wives with no inkling that women had a say. Violence and brutality were the stock market of the day—the more you had, the higher you climbed. Things got so bad that—to borrow from my gamer kids'—God had to reformat the system or risk losing the entire thing.

For the non-computer nerds here, whenever a PC gets a really bad virus (apparently the worst virus ever created is called the "I Love You" virus) you have two options. You can either allow the virus to affect your computer until it becomes unusable, and you have to discard it, or you reformat the system wiping out the virus—and sadly all your cat pictures with it. But at least, you save the system and can start over.

Well God didn't choose either option. Instead, he went for a kind of half-reformat. We know this because God didn't wipe out humanity. Through Noah and his family, God kept the species alive. It's likely that without this reset, the entire species would have wiped itself out. So, through the ark, God preserved the species and slowed the effects of the virus. But because the virus lives inside of people, Noah and his family became the very means by which the virus remained. In short, God slowed the spread of the virus and saved the species, but the virus was still there.

Not long after the flood, the virus is back at it again. The people at the time gathered together to build a great city and tower that reached the heavens. Without getting too detailed here, whatever was going on in this story it was bad. God loves it when people work together to accomplish great things—it was his original plan. But when those people are the Nazis, and the great things are actually terrible things, oneness becomes a means to unprecedented evil as opposed to good. And apparently, whatever the folk at Babel were up to was existentially threatening enough that God had to intervene.

God confused the languages of the people so they couldn't work together. He then scattered the people across the earth. The scattered peoples went from Babel to establish new nations and empires—most of which worshipped all kinds of false gods. In fact, the Bible goes a step beyond this by saying that God handed the scattered post-Babel peoples over to false gods. These fallen beings (demons) were the inheritance of the nations that spread out after Babel. Why? Because not a single post-Babel society was friends of YHWH. So, God handed them over to false gods. (Deut. 4:19-20; 32:8)

Because idolatry and social injustice are always linked together, many of these nations engineered new systems (religious and political) that thrived on exploitation (rich over poor), human merchandise and commodification (temple prostitutes), and crimes against humanity (slavery, patriarchy, child sacrifice) etc. (Psalm 82) It looked as though, once again, the virus was eating up the species.

But God had a plan. One of the families to emerge from the post-Babel world was the family of a man named Abram. Now Abram wasn't exactly the cream of the human crop. He was a deeply flawed, patriarchal, self-protecting chump who risked his wife's safety in order to save his own neck (you know, that whole "tell Pharaoh you're my sister so he doesn't kill me to get you" even though it meant Sarai was likely going to end up in Pharaoh's bed.)

But through this flawed man and his family, God promised he would birth an entirely new and unheard-of nation—a new people, a new society and civilisation: *The nation of Israel.* Although the inheritance of the other nations were false gods (Deut. 32:8), Israels inheritance was to be YHWH himself. (Deut. 32:9) And through this new nation, God intended to regather the scattered peoples bringing all the nations back into relationship with himself.

Now don't miss the main point here.

God's plan for Abram's descendants was HUGE.

Through Abram, God was going to birth an entirely new people—a new nation, a new society, a new civilisation that would operate according to entirely new social structures intended to engineer a kingdom that was socially just, economically altruistic, legally honest, and spiritually pure.

In a post-Babel world of dog-eat-dog nations that reflected the selfish nature of their gods, YHWH birthed a new nation to reflect the selfless nature of his heart. And through this new nation, God told Abram "All the nations of the earth will be blessed." (Genesis 22:18)

In other words, Israel was not meant to be an exclusive club for the religious elite. It was meant to be a portal for all people, all nations, and all tribes. Anyone from any of the fallen, idolatrous, post-Babel nations who craved the beauty of God reflected through his people would be welcomed into the family.

But don't miss the cosmo-political significance of this. If this new nation is the means by which God will reclaim all the nations of the earth, then the gods who govern those other nations (demons) would see Israel as their greatest threat. They would stop at nothing to destroy it.

Here is a quick summary to keep things aligned:

CREATION	BABEL	ISRAEL
God creates humans and places them in a garden to be his representatives. God's aim is to populate the earth in partnership with people. Had God's	Humanity rebels and is cast out of the garden. Wickedness spreads so God hits the reset button (flood). After the flood, humanity rebels	God chooses a man out of the post-Babel scatter—Abram. Through Abram, God promises to create a new nation through whom he will redeem

plan gone on without a hitch, humanity would have lived as a global village, united in their love of God and each other for all eternity.	again, so God confuses the languages and scatters them. The scattered nations are under the authority of fallen gods.	the rest of the scattered nations. Israel is not to be an exclusive nation but an inclusive people inviting the scattered nations back.

The story continues:

While it took a bit longer, Israel—like the post-Babel nations—turned its back on YHWH and began worshipping the same false gods that governed the scattered nations. And sure enough, as they did so, the new nation abandoned its selfless social systems for oppressive and unjust ones. In time, this new civilisation became more wicked than the idolatrous nations that surrounded them. Things got so bad; the book of Chronicles tells us the streets of Jerusalem flowed with the blood of the innocents. Judges could be bought with bribes, so the poor had no hope of justice against the rich. And the politicians were constantly seeking alliances with other corrupt nations.

In a last-ditch effort to preserve his people, God sent them into exile. But things didn't get much better after. While the post-exile generations turned away from idolatry, they went too far in the opposite direction. A spirit of sectarianism and arrogance took over. Rather than a welcoming committee for God, they became bouncers blocking the way to his kingdom. Apart from the remnant God preserved, Israel's original calling as a never-before-seen nation in friendship with God and a portal through whom all the other nations would be included in the blessings of Abraham had been abandoned.

It is in this context that Jesus appears. And as we will see in more detail in the next chapter, all of Jesus' activity points to one thing: *he is engineering a new Israel.*[17]

Through the outcasts, the marginalised, and the misfits Jesus is gathering and crafting a new society. The sermon on the mount is more than just a sermon. It is a new social structure, a new way of living and being in the world. The twelve apostles are the new tribes of this new Israel. And instead of a physical temple in its midst, this new Israel is itself the temple. The people, filled with the Spirit of God, are the temple God has always wanted.

And of course, this new Israel was to continue the original mission of drawing all the scattered peoples back into oneness with God. This new Israel was to reclaim the essence of a new society, a new civilisation, and a new community never-before-seen on the earth.

This new Israel is the church. An identity, a new way of governance, a new social rhythm, a new ethic, and society—NOT a 2-hour Sabbath morning event.

Now notice this (it's pretty epic): As soon as the church takes off in Pentecost (Acts 1), the first thing God does is pour out his Spirit into his new temple-made-of-people (*ekklesia*, church). But what God does is weird.

[17] Bear in mind that the use of the term "New Israel" in this book is to be understood biblically and not as an affirmation of replacement theology. In scripture "new" means "original". In this sense, the New Israel is really the original Israel God had in mind. It is a Jewish phenomenon which grafts in the Gentiles from the fallen nations to create one united human family in Christ.

The Spirit appears as fire. But notice that the fire is described as "tongues" that give the apostles the supernatural ability to communicate the gospel in languages they had never learned.

Why?

The answer is simple: the church is the new Israel, tasked with gathering to itself all the post-Babel nations scattered about the earth. Through the Spirit, God intends his new Israel, the church, to be the literal and tangible reversal of the curse of Babel.

The church is the new society through whom God will restore the scattered nations back into relationship with himself.

Wow.

And of course, just as Israel presented the greatest threat to fallen gods in the OT, the new Israel presents the greatest threat in the new. The church now has the target on its back. Spiritually corrupt forces would stop at nothing to destroy it.

A quick summary before moving on:

EXILE	JESUS	SPIRIT
Israel was God's chosen nation to bring everyone back into oneness with himself. But Israel also rebelled against God. They became more wicked than the pagan nations around them. God eventually judged Israel, sending it into	When Jesus comes, the religious leaders have cultivated an exclusive, judgmental community that rejects sinners. So, Jesus begins creating a new Israel—and he does so through the very sinners the religious leaders reject. This new Israel	In Pentecost, the Holy Spirit is poured out on the church. And the first sign of his presence is the reversal of the curse of Babel. No longer separated by confused languages, the church can now fulfil Israel's mission of creating, from all the nations a

exile in Babylon as a means of preserving it.	of Jesus is the church—a new society.	new, unheard-of people.

This is some pretty epic stuff. But before we wrap up, notice what God gives this new Israel in order to accomplish its radically wild mission. He gives them his Spirit to dwell in each of them (and not in a special building). And it is through this mobile nation filled with the fire of God that God planned to regather the scattered peoples of the world back into a new post-human family—the church.

This counter-Babel mission is what God is up to in the world. This new Israel, new society and new kingdom transcends all temporal social walls of separation. In this new family, all are one in Jesus. This is God's secret, *hidden* plan. And through it, he would bring the history of rebellion and separation to its end.

What Happened?

So, if the church is literally a foretaste of the new society of heaven, a new nation and culture all together, then how did it come to be reduced to little more than an event we attend each weekend?

Because despite the amazing things we have explored so far, one this is clear: today, the story is essentially the opposite. We have money. Lots of it. We have buildings. Tons of them. We run programs. So many of them. Our events are often impressive and logistically complex. But we are struggling.

I believe the answer is simple. The church, just like Israel, is not merely another nation or group of people. It is literally God's main weapon for reclaiming the scattered nations—under the dominion of fallen gods—back to himself. In other words, we are the means through which God snatches the captives from Satan's kingdom. What this means is that the church is dangerous because it is in open conflict with fallen gods who have a vested interest in keeping their captives.

Think about it. When speaking of the church, Jesus said that the "the gates of Hades (Hell) will not prevail against it." (Matthew 16:18) Most of the time when we quote this verse, we tend to imagine that Hell is attacking the church, but God protects it from all of Hell's satanic advances.

But look again. That's not what the verse is saying. Jesus says, the "*gates* of hell will not prevail." Gates don't attack. They defend. Which means in Jesus' mind, Hell is not attacking but defending. It's the church that's on the attack. It's the church that's on the offensive. Why? Because the scattered nations were given over to false gods. God handed them over because of their rebellion. But he never intended for them to stay there. Through Israel, and now the church, God has birthed a new people with one task—*to get the captives back*.

And so, the church attacks. It tears down the walls of Hell. It crushes its gates and unhinges them. And the church pours in. Into the city. Into the neighbourhood. Unrestricted. Undeterred. An unstoppable force of love, community, and connection. And as the fallen nations see this, as they see Jesus in us and through us, their hearts are awakened, the veil is lifted, the spell of the enemy is broken, and they are drawn by the rhythms of God's love. The prophet Isaiah put it this way,

> [God] will destroy the covering which is over all peoples, The veil which is stretched over all nations. (Isaiah 25:7)

Because of this, you can only imagine that the enemy would be hard at work ensuring the church would stray away from its grand purpose. And if he couldn't destroy the church, he would distract it.

Church history shows us that distraction won the day. As the church gained political and social power, it gradually sold itself out from a new, trans-terrestrial Kingdom to the glue of the Roman empire.

Other complex changes were taking place as well. Among those changes came the distinction between "clergy" and "laity." The laity (ordinary people) were no longer priests in a new nation, but attendees at weekly *events* (the mass) where the "clergy" (the holy ones with access to God) could confer special blessings and grace on them.

Traditions came to replace the organic movement of the church. Cathedrals replaced homes. Priests replaced priesthood. And the supremacy of the Roman empire was conflated with the church to such an extent, the new humanity and new kingdom was lost sight of, completely subsumed by the temporal agendas of Rome's political aspirations.

The protestant reformation resisted some of what the church had become. But in many ways, it remained the same. The philosopher Soren Kierkegaard decried how Christendom had morphed into little more than a social statement, church attendance emerging as a cultural convention necessary for local reputation and prestige. There was no supernatural love, no new Israel, no alternate community living counterculturally on the earth. Only actors and performers attending religious events in order to tick the necessary boxes required for good social standing.

To this day, little has changed. For most of us, church is an event we attend, not a new civilisation we belong to. We see one another at the weekend event but have virtually zero connection during the week. We organise programs, roster people for events, and perform our duties with zeal. But once the event is over, we go back to our own little worlds completely detached from community.

In almost every way, modern Adventists behave like club members. We show up, do our thing, pay our dues, and wave farewell until the next event. This is not how a new society living out the rhythms of a new kingdom in relational, interconnected ways looks. This is what a bowling club does. And even then, they often do it better.

Are all churches like this? No. Do all our members have an experience like the above? No. There are certainly exceptions. But those exceptions don't break the norm. In Australia, the national low for SDA churches (according to the Natural Church Development survey) was "loving relationships." In the USA, the stats are much the same.

We are good at many things—being an alternative community that gathers the scattered nations back into a single-family defined by the love of Jesus? That we're not so good at. Recent surveys and census data across the west is clear—fewer and fewer people identify with any organised religion or church. The new community Jesus founded as the reversal of Babel, the phenomenon God designed to attract all peoples to himself, has become the very thing that repels.

So where do we go from here? The answer is found in the unfolding narrative of scripture. Let's keep exploring.

CHAPTER 9

HUMAN

Most Christians today—and certainly most Adventists—have a certain mental picture of the church. It often contains three chief ingredients. The first is the building, which we have already explored. The second is the gathering event—which we also touched on in the last chapter. And the third is the Sabbath main morning program.

This program has become so central to how the church sees itself that it has become fundamentally synonymous with its identity. So much so that when people think of "church" or speak of "going to church" what they generally mean is the Sabbath morning service, which in some places is referred to as the "divine service", the "main service" or the "sacred hour."

With phrases like that, one would think that this Sabbath morning program is something God explicitly commanded in scripture and absolutely central to the nature and identity of the biblical church. But here is where things get strange. Scour the NT from cover to cover, read everything you can possibly read about the early church, and you will never, not once, find anything remotely close to our modern-day church programs.

In this sense, almost everything that happens on a typical Sabbath morning church service is not in the Bible. Even the very concept of the service itself is foreign to the NT.

But didn't the early Christians meet to fellowship, worship, pray and be in the word? Isn't that a 'church service' like what we see today?

Great question. I get this one all the time. In fact, every single time I discuss the non-Biblical nature of our programs, this question comes up. And here is my answer:

Yes and No.

For example, the early church did worship together, and pray, and fellowship and spend time in the word—chiefly in small groups scattered about the city. They also discipled others, did evangelism, acts of service and compassion, and spread the gospel.

And if this is all we did in our church gatherings, that would be great.

But it isn't.

1.

First, we have already seen that the early church did these things daily. Living out the kingdom was not something they reserved for some special program at the end of the week. It was an everyday rhythm. This meant their entire lives were re-authored, re-prioritised and reoriented toward this kingdom rhythm. It wasn't an event you set aside two special hours to run. It was a way of life that completely reshaped your everyday habits, patterns, postures, and pursuits. This re-forming of a person's life was not reserved to professional clergy, either. *All the believers did this.*

2.

Second, the early church did this in small groups scattered about various regions where everyone could participate. There was no big church building where 100 people turned up to listen to one person talk, one person pray, and one person sing a "special item" on a stage while 90% of the attendants merely consumed and observed for 2 hours. The groups were small so that everyone could use their gift and participate in the gathering, offering prayers, praises, and words of encouragement. The closest thing you got to a sermon was when an Apostle's letter arrived, and they were read out loud to everyone and discussed. In short, a "church service" in the early church was a group of believers all serving one another and their community daily, not a large group of people coming to a building in order to be served by a small contingent of church program organisers.

3.

Third, let's be honest here. While we do some of the same things the early church did, our services have way more to do with suits, ties, 3-hymn sandwiches, the lectern (where sermonising takes place), and Eurocentric cultural expressions than anything else. If you doubt this, try showing up to preach with no tie and see how many people flip out. Never mind that most of our churches have little to no real fellowship and community. Forget the fact that Jesus commanded us to love one another as he loved us. And let's also ignore the way in which the early church served its local community passionately (something most of our local churches never do). None of these things (what the Bible actually commands) will cause a stir or a commotion in the church. Showing up without a tie? That will do it. (PS. I get that not every SDA church is like this, but after years of lay and pastoral ministry in various parts of the world, I have found this to be the norm.)

The truth is, it's the stuff the Bible doesn't command that we get worked up over, not the stuff it does command. The early church met primarily in homes. They ate together, worshipped, and prayed in small groups, and had no age-segregated ministries, 3-hymn sandwiches, suits and ties, or a lectern with weekly sermons on a stage (we call it a pulpit to make it sound holier, but it's a stage).

Their gatherings were a lot more informal, down-to-earth, and human. There were no pews, no stained-glass windows, no elevated stage, no bulletins, and no minute-by-minute order of service. Instead, they had meals, a table, open arms, and a willingness to lay down their lives for others.

So, when people say the church service today is exactly what the NT describes, I have no clue what they are talking about. It's not exactly like it at all. And in fact, it's the stuff that the Bible doesn't mention or command that we seem most willing to go to war over. Our idolatry of tradition and our commitment to bygone Eurocentric cultural expressions seems to be a lot more important and central to Adventist identity than is loving one another (a command that appears 59 times in the NT).

So, what is the solution? How do we recover a Biblical picture and practice of "church" that is invigorating and meaningful—especially in our post-church age? The answer to that question is multi-layered, but for now, we can keep it simple. Let's return to the narrative of scripture and allow it to unfold, opening our eyes to the mystery of the church. With a Biblical foundation, we will have more clarity on where to go next.

What The Church Is

Before we begin, I have to be honest. This chapter is a bit long. At the same time, it's way too short. What I mean is, even though it's long the topics I must cover are so huge, this part of the book could easily be 10 times longer. But I'm not going to do that to you. Instead, I am aiming to keep this as simple and precise as possible. So here is an outline of what we will explore and bring together. Each of these headings are super essential to fully appreciating the mystery of the church:

1. The nature and purpose of Israel.
2. The offensiveness of the New Israel.
3. The mystery of a New Humanity.

We will briefly touch on all 3 of these, and then bring them all together before we close. To begin, let's head back to our prime text:

> Have the people of Israel build me a holy sanctuary so I can live among them. (Exodus 25:8)

The Nature and Purpose of Israel

We have looked at the above text a number of times with a special focus on the "dwell" or "live among" parts. In this chapter, I want to focus on the "them" being spoken of.

This "them" is God's specially chosen nation—Israel. God has asked this chosen people to build a sanctuary for him so that he could dwell among them in a way that no other people on earth can enjoy. They are a chosen people, especially set apart for closeness with God.

However, God wasn't playing favourites here. Israel's job as a "chosen nation" was to reveal the heart of God to the surrounding nations. Their task was to partner with God in drawing the other nations back to friendship with him.

In short, Israel was not chosen *from* the world so much as it was chosen *for* the world.

Their true call was to be an invitational people who not only reflected the heart of God to the pagan nations but whose posture was inclusive and welcoming. Israel, then, were ambassadors handing out invitations to God's house, not bouncers blocking the door to his presence.

However, fast-forward to the post-exilic period, and a new generation was so bent on manifesting full, inflexible, unbending obedience to God that they became a radically exclusive community who saw all others as spiritual viruses to avoid for fear of contamination. Only the circumcised descendants of Abraham were loved by God. All others were birth rejects.

Yes, a foreigner could convert to Judaism, but they were always considered second-class. Likewise, sinful or suffering members of Israelite society were considered to have done something so bad (or their parents) that God had chosen to ignore their Abrahamic heritage and reject them anyway.

So, in the end, you had to be a religiously upright, socially respectable member of the Abrahamic family tree to be considered one of the truly chosen and truly worthy.

The Offensiveness of the New Israel.

Against this backdrop, Jesus shows up and begins his ministry by preaching a sermon that almost got him killed. What could he have possibly preached? We find the story in Luke 4:

> The Spirit of the Lord is on me, because he has anointed me to proclaim good news to the poor. He has sent me to proclaim freedom for the prisoners and recovery of sight for the blind, to set the oppressed free, to proclaim the year of the Lord's favor. (Luke 4:18-19)

Notice what Jesus is saying in his sermon: *I am here for the poor, the blind, and the oppressed*. In short, all the people rejected by the religious class as unloved and unworthy and sinful. But it gets worse. Jesus then says this:

> [T]here were many widows in Israel in Elijah's time, when the sky was shut for three and a half years and there was a severe famine throughout the land. Yet Elijah was not sent to any of them, but to a widow in Zarephath in the region of Sidon. And there were many in Israel with leprosy in the time of Elisha the prophet, yet not one of them was cleansed—only Naaman the Syrian. (Luke 4:25-27)

Follow this closely now. Jesus has not only announced that he is there, on God's behalf, for the outcasts of Israel—he is also there for the birth rejects in the pagan nations.

In fact, God has always been searching for them. So, Jesus has just told his audience of religiously zealous Israelites that he is not there for them, he is there for the outcasts of Israel and the pagan rejects.

Needless to say, that really ticked them off.

This theme repeats over and over again in the book of Luke. Jesus starts his mission of "spiritual liberation" and immediately we see him healing a demon-possessed man, then a leper, and then a paralytic. During this time, Jesus picks 12 apostles, none of whom would be picked by our nominating committees to lead any ministries (except maybe Judas), and among them is a conman/ tax collector named Levi.

Levi then throws a party and invites all his shady friends. And while Jesus and his disciples are there partying, the religious leaders show up and ask, "Why do you eat and drink with such scum?" (5:30), to which Jesus replied, "I haven't come for the righteous, but for sinners." (32)

But perhaps the most offensive part of all of this is how Jesus organises and frames his entire ministry. He begins by liberating sinners from their oppression, then he calls 12 apostles to be his inner circle, and then he preaches "the sermon on the mount" (chapter 6) in which he proclaims the way of the new kingdom.

What is Jesus doing here? To the religious Jewish mind, it's super obvious. *Jesus is re-enacting the book of Exodus where God liberated Israel from Egypt, organised it under its 12 tribes, and led them to a mountain to proclaim his way*.

To make it dummy-proof, here is what's happening: Jesus is creating a new Israel—and guess what? He is populating his new Israel—not with the religious elite—but with outcasts, pagans, and rejects.

Ouch.

But why is Jesus creating a New Israel for the misfits?

Because his kingdom was always meant to be for everyone. From the beginning of time until now, God has been longing to heal all of humanity and restore us to closeness with himself. We are all sinners, all separated from the father, all in need of an invitation and grace. We are united in our fallenness, and therefore, all invited to the table.

The Mystery of a New Humanity

But this raises another question. What's the point of this invitation? I mean, we get God loves sinners. But is there something more? The answer is yes. Every human to ever live has lived in a fallen, sinful state. But then Jesus comes—God in human flesh—and in that body he engineers a new kind of human who lives and breathes the rhythms of divine love. And every fallen child of Adam, whether Jew or not, is invited into this new humanity.

This was Jesus' mission all along. That in him, there is a new human, and now he invites all of us into this new humanity, this new way, a new civilisation, a new society, and a new species restored to harmony with the way of other-centred love. This new humanity is a new family and belongs, not to the family of Adam, but to the family of Jesus. He is the ancestor of an entirely new species in which man and divinity intertwine in relational intimacy. And this new species is so radical, that none of the old categories of human existence count anymore. Not gender, not class, not culture. Thus, Paul the Apostle could say,

> There is neither Jew nor Gentile, neither slave nor free, nor is there male and female, for you are all one in Christ Jesus. (Galatians 3:28)

And here's the bottom line, you guys. This new humanity, this new family, is grafted together from all corners of the earth into a New Israel defined, not by the biological DNA of Abraham, but by his *Spiritual DNA*—that is, his faith.

So, in the end, what you discover is Jesus is creating a Spiritual Israel populated by a Spiritual People who have been Spiritually Reborn and are now defined by a Spiritual DNA through whom he is constructing a Spiritual Temple all over the earth.

This new Israel, new humanity, new temple phenomenon that transcends all physical boundaries, tribal borders and cultural limitations is the *church.*

But it gets crazier. According to Paul, the NT church isn't merely a new humanity, new temple phenomenon living out the beauty of God on the earth. The NT church is also a program that takes place on a stage.

Wait, what?

Didn't I start out by saying that the NT church did not have any programs or any stages? That these are modern phenomenon that are not part of the church's primitive DNA?

Yes, I did say that. However, follow with me here. Because it turns out the church *is*, indeed, a program on a stage. Paul explains this in Ephesians 3:10 when he says that God's purpose, in the church, is that this group of new humans would reveal the richness and wisdom of God "to the rulers and authorities in the heavenly realms".

Wait, what?

Take a few deep breaths as this sinks in:

1. The church *is* a program on a stage.
2. The stage is the earth, and the program is people, living real lives, in real communities and neighbourhoods, with real love and grace in their hearts, flooding their cities with the richness of God.
3. And as they do this, a host of trans-terrestrial, alter-dimensional beings observe to see the beauty of God on display.

This means the church is a protagonist in a cosmic theatre that displays to spiritual beings in other dimensions the goodness of God's heart.

This new Israel, new humanity, new temple phenomenon that transcends all cultural limitations is immersed in a cosmic theatrical drama unfolding before the eyes of spiritual intelligences.

And this demonstration of the goodness of God is not displayed through our reductionist, compartmentalised programs in our cosmically unimpressive buildings with our strait-jacket traditions.

It is displayed through real people, in real communities, living real lives that flood their city with the goodness of God, spreading the fire of his Spirit from family to family and home to home in such a radical way it blows the minds of divine beings who inhabit spiritual dimensions.

And this, ladies, and gentlemen—THIS is the great mystery.

Now we can begin to appreciate, ever so slightly, the depths of what God had hidden for generations. The church is the gathering of this new species never before seen in the universe until Jesus. He is the first of its kind. The first human in history to live in harmony with the heart of God, even through torture and death. This new humanity transcends all barriers and lines of demarcation imposed on us by society and empire. This new humanity is like Jesus—not in a perfectionist behaviourally obsessed sense—but in a rhythmic, harmonic sense. A new society of people defined, not by power struggles and arbitrary categories, but by other-centred love so radical, it amazes the principalities and powers in heavenly places.

And it is through this love that Jesus repeatedly said, the world would come to know him.

Not prophecy seminars, great church programs, clever events or brilliant marketing/ media.

But a new humanity living out the rhythms of self-sacrificing love for one another. A new humanity composed of everyone—male, female, Jew, gentile, rich, poor, slave, free—all serving one another and laying their lives down for each other.

And this great mystery is meant to flood the earth, home by home, family by family, building the spiritual temple from one neighbourhood to the next, inviting the scattered nations away from the fallen gods that oppress them and into the new family defined by its radical other-centred, Christ-like love. A family that models the way of the new human, not through special programs we attend for 2-hours a week but through daily life on life connection with our cities.

What Happened?

When the church became a program in a building, it moved away from a new humanity in which each member served each other and their community to a spectator event in which each attendee is conditioned to consume and receive. With this model of church in place, we will never see a revival of the new humanity, and we will never see a return to the primitive rhythms that made the early church the force that it was. The two are simply not compatible with one another. Either the building with the program is the main thing, or missional living in active discipleship communities committed to the rhythms of the new humanity are the thing. We cannot have both.

But how did we move so far from the original plan? As I mentioned in the previous chapter, how the church shifted from this earth-shattering mystery to its present form is a long, messy, and incredibly complex conversation. There are lots of moving pieces and if I tried to cover them here, this book would become a dissertation.

But here is a "nutshell version" in 3 simple points.

1. As we reach the later centuries of Christianity, the church came to adopt a "sacramental" theology. What this means is, the church began to teach that while grace is free, it can only be administered via the institution and its approved priests. The church basically became a petrol station of grace. You could

only get grace through it, and even then, you needed weekly top-ups. The places where these top-ups happened were in the church buildings/ cathedrals. The priests alone had the power to administer grace—mainly through things like the weekly mass, confession, and baptism—all of which took place exclusively in the building. Thus, the building became the "house of God", the place where his presence dwelled and the only place where his grace could be accessed. This theological shift obliterated the beautiful house-to-house, family-to-family, fire-spreading movement of the early church. It siphoned all the Christians into centralised events where they could do little more than observe and receive.

2. The protestant reformation sought a return to scripture, but they only went so far. Instead of returning to the table, the weekly mass was replaced by the weekly sermon. And being that the protestant reformation took place during the same time as the scientific revolution, there was a growing passion and interest in robust, rational discourse. As a result, the lectern became the new centre of church life. Add the fact that many people had never heard the Bible expounded upon in any practical or systematic sense, and you can see why this was so appealing.

3. Fast-forward to today, and the innovations of the reformation have become mere formalities. Every week we do the same thing—Sabbath school lesson and sermon, over and over again. Factor in the modern obsession with consumerism, and you have before you the modern church—a religious event that revolves around services and programs where

we come to "be served" rather than serve others.

Every week, church leaders have to invest energy in putting on the best program possible and people walk in, expecting a good spiritual performance. If it's not up to par, we complain that we "weren't fed", that the music was subpar, that the youth are singing new songs, that the preacher didn't wear a tie, that the sermon wasn't theologically accurate enough and so on.

Forgive me for being so forward, but I don't think we have enough time left in earth's history to beat around the bush. So let me get right to it.

How many more sermons do we need to hear before we choose to go do something? How many more Bible studies do we need to join before we decide to go love someone? How many more programs, events, and services do we need to attend before we accept that we have heard enough, know enough, and now it's time to go serve somebody?

We're so good at the programs and events, but do we know the practical step-by-step skills for effective missional living? Do we know what it looks like to love radically? Do we reflect a new humanity that moves to the rhythms of love in such a mind-blowing way that people wonder what is going on? Are we lighting our communities and cities ablaze by spreading the fire of the Spirit from one family and one home to another? Do we live as temples and priests in whom people can encounter the presence of God?

No. We are more concerned with our programs and dogmatic "standards"—most of which come from European cultural expressions and not the Bible (suits, ties, hymns, KJV bibles, Victorian social conventions, and expectations, etc).

We get more upset if the pastor doesn't wear a suit than we do with the fact that our church doesn't know any of its neighbours. We go to war with the youth and their new ideas, but sit idly by while the church withers and dies with no relevant impact in its community.

In short, we have become a people who don't care about what Jesus cares about. We only care about what we care about. And what we care about is insultingly, and ridiculously frivolous and measly and small.

We are no longer a new species living out the rhythms of a new humanity and bringing to our tables the outcast and the ostracised. Instead, we are the ones determining who the outcast and ostracised are.

Jesus was called a friend of sinners. The church is more like a bouncer. We welcome sinners, sure—but only the ones that are close enough to our cultural shape that we can easily mould them into our social script.

So, when the world thinks of the church, they don't see anything close to what people saw when Jesus was here. Instead of a table for the outcast, the church has become a private club for the religious elite—the ones who dress the right way, talk the right way, and believe the right things.

Everyone else is on the out.

Conclusion

There is a lot more I could say, but this chapter has gone on long enough. So, I am going to stop here. But I don't want to leave you wading in the depths of the negative and the bad. There is good news. Incredibly good news. In Jesus, there is another way. God has not left us to our own self-sabotaging devices. His grace extends, even to us, and even now.

We will explore what this looks like in the coming chapters.

CHAPTER 10

WONDER

One of ministry's most stressful burdens is "church growth." Conferences and pastors are often obsessed with this topic because let's face it, none of us wants to see "church death." We want thriving churches that are impacting their communities and reaching their neighbours. And of course, all of this translates to more people attending church, getting baptised, and joining the mission. When a church is healthy and active, it is growing. When it is insular and sickly, it is dying.

I have shared this burden for much of my ministry. In the early days, church growth was my number one passion. And why not? If you love the gospel and the great commission, then church growth should be one of your top goals as a believer. After all, the book of Acts is full of reports of thousands being added to the church here and thousands there. The book of Revelation also celebrates the multitudes of the saved whose numbers are so vast, John says they can't be counted. So, if God is into numbers—including numbers so big humans can't calculate them—we should be too.

To a certain degree, I still hold these convictions. I want to see our church thrive—it's why I wrote this book. And by thrive, I mean I want to see it make a meaningful impact in the world through the power of the gospel and grow as a result. After all, the church is the family of God—and God likes big families.

However, the conversation over church growth—while often stemming from a good place—can easily devolve into something far from good. This leads me to the main "church is not" theme I want to focus on in this chapter.

The church is NOT a business.[18]

What do I mean here? Let me keep this as simple as possible. When the mission of the church gets reduced to KPIs (key performance indicators), numerical targets, process optimisation, and productivity hacks designed to maximise product output (like baptisms or bums-on-seats) it becomes more like a factory conveyor belt and less like the sacred mystery that it is.

Over time, running the church becomes no different to running a well-oiled corporation that revolves around branding, marketing, sales funnels, conversion gimmicks, and customer satisfaction. With a church model like this, you are guaranteed to have results and baptise many—but it comes at a profound cost. The more businesslike the church becomes the less remains of its *wonder*.

Now don't get me wrong. I'm all for good stewardship of our limited resources, including time, finances, and energy. The proper administration of these requires logistical artistry, well-

[18] It's important to point out that as I challenge church business culture, I am keeping my focus on how local churches function and operate. This is not a critique of Adventism's global institutional structure nor is it a critique of order, strategies, and administrative layers overall. First, global critiques go beyond the scope of this book which focuses its attention on the local church. Second, anti-order or anti-structure are not positions that I hold nor encourage. I explore this topic more in chapter 12.

designed plans, and intentional strategies. But if we are not careful, we might arrive at a Laodicean state of affairs—one in which we no longer need the Holy Spirit because we have our church growth gurus, hacks, and models. And so long as we tick the boxes in the church manual or the latest church growth system trending in Christian bookstores, then we can pull off what appears to be a pretty successful church.

But the early church was nothing like this. Sure, it was in its infancy and would eventually mature and grow in ways not present in the book of Acts. But the foundational principles of the church are there, and they are timeless. While we can certainly build on these principles, the moment we start operating against them we are no longer building the church of scripture. We are building something else entirely. And if there is one thing that is clear from the NT church is that it was not a business—it was a community of people filled with the spirit who lived the incarnational life of Jesus in their cities. It was not a building. It was not a show. It was not a program. It was not a performance. It was not a club. It was not an institution. It was a wonder. A wonder of divine presence, relational passion, and communal oneness that changed the world.

But the church changed. And few have captured the hilarity of its tragic shifts better than US Senate Chaplain, Dr. Richard C. Halverson when he said:

> In the first century in Palestine, Christianity was a community of believers. Then Christianity moved to Greece and became a philosophy. Then it moved to Rome and became an institution. Then it moved to Europe and became a culture.

> And then it moved to America and became a business.

While Halverson's quip is humorous, it is likewise nested with complexity and weight. All of the shifts that have remoulded and redefined the church over the centuries appeared justifiable and necessary at the time—and this includes the shift to a business model.

Now let's be fair here. Most proponents of the business model would argue that before it came into focus, churches were dying everywhere. The love of tradition, the dry hum of the status quo, and the lack of social and practical engagement with the world meant most churches were aging and fading. Worse yet, few people seemed to care. It was in this context that a handful of forward-thinking, innovative, entrepreneurial mavericks began to reshape the church using business models—and it worked. Churches started to grow again.

But it came at a cost.

In 2007, one of the leading "business" model churches in the world, Willowcreek Community Church, repented of its program-driven approach with the cryptic words, "We made a mistake."[19] People were attending church and participating in all kinds of activities, but they were not being discipled and not growing into mature and obedient followers of Christ.

I wish the problem with this business model ended there. But it doesn't. The gospel became a product, discipleship became a sales funnel, evangelism became a copywriting technique, and

---

[19] Christianity Today. "Willow Creek Repents?" (Web: www.christianitytoday.com)

evangelistic campaigns sounded more like clickbait, infomercials, and scripts from an NLP (Neurological Language Patterns) marketing course than genuine invitations to faith in Jesus.

In time, the business model developed churches with incredible branding, cultural influence, and pastoral celebrities, but beneath the shiny exterior, things were beginning to rust.

Lead pastor of Willowcreek, Bill Hybels, resigned as he came under investigation for sexual abuse. Other celebrity pastors like Bruxey Cavey, Mark Driscoll, Carl Lentz, Brian Houston, and Matthew Chandler met the same fate. The once powerful multisite "Mars Hill" church collapsed and the once globally influential and culturally awe-inspiring "Hillsong" brand tumbled shortly after.

The age of the CEO pastor produced incredible business models that put the church back in motion, but its collateral effect was anything but positive. Men in positions of celebrity-like influence they should never have held abused their power and prestige leaving behind them a trail of wounded and hurting souls. And the churches, built like businesses, responded with Public Relations campaigns. Their main goal appeared to be the protection and preservation of their "brand" rather than the healing and restoration of the hurting. [20]

---

[20] It's important to point out that none of these scandals are new. We see the same (and worse) scandals in conservative/ traditional churches that often reject business models. We also see these scandals all throughout Christian history. The point here is not that a business model creates this culture, but that it perpetuates it with ease. Church as philosophy, as empire, as culture, and as business all seem to fuel the same issues. Church as a simple community is not a magical fix, but it helps create healthier environments within which safe church cultures can emerge.

I wish I could remember where I saw this so I could provide proper attribution, but somewhere on Instagram I ran into one of the most insightful questions regarding clergy and church leadership abuse scandals that went something like this:

> Are we witnessing church scandals? Or is this just church culture?

I would argue, it is church culture. Although it's been this way long before the business model showed up (Dark Ages anyone?) we can't deny that this modern iteration has perpetuated a celebrity, performative, and power-lusting monster that—for all its temporal benefits—has left a trail of hurting people in its wake.

I could go on about this for pages to come. But here's my main point: no matter how justified it might have appeared; *the church is not a business*. It is infinitely more. It is a mystery of wonder so sublime that the chief metaphor used of it in scripture is the image of a "bride" who is on her way to wed the eternal Creator.

To reduce the bride of Christ to a brand with a logo and a membership roll is among the modern church's greatest and most tragic blunders.

What The Church Is

Let's switch gears and dig deeper into what the church is. To do so, I will first explain a little thing called "Game Theory" introduced by scholar James P. Carse. I want to use this concept as an illustration that will help us see a more biblical and radical picture of the church—one that retains its sacred wonder without denying its responsibility for growth and success.

First, let's define terms. In the article, "Are you playing a finite game, or an infinite one?" the author quotes Carse's own definition of finite games:

> [F]inite games [are games] which have a definite beginning and ending, and are bounded by specific rules.[21]

In other words, a finite game is the everyday kind of game you are already familiar with. Things like baseball, pool, spades, and chess—all of these are finite games. They have specific players with specific rules and a specific outcome. Another way of understanding a finite game is that, in essence, "[a] finite game is played to win."

But what about an infinite game? That one is a bit tougher to understand. Kevin Kelly provides a neat definition in his article, "Playing the Infinite Game."[22]

> An infinite game, on the other hand, is played to keep the game going. It does not terminate because there is no winner. An infinite game, however, can keep going only by changing its rules.[23]

---

[21] Hollingworth, Patrick. "Are you Playing a Finite Game or an Infinite One?" (Web: patrickhollingworth.com)
[22] Kelley, Kevin. "Playing the Infinite Game." (Web: realitysandwich.com)
[23] *ibid.*

Some examples of infinite games are things like politics. There isn't a winner or loser in politics. No one ever takes home the politics trophy. Instead, people come and go into the game. They play for as long as they can, and then they drop out and others take their place. There aren't set rules either. Instead, the rules change and evolve to accommodate societal shifts and at times, to lead those societal shifts.

The same can be said for the stock market. There are no set players. They come and go. There are no set rules, they shift as well. Education is also an infinite game. It evolves over time as new developments come to light. No one ever wins that game. It's infinite. It never ends and the rules just keep changing. Culture, philosophy, business, empire, fashion—all of these are examples of infinite games.

But why does this matter and what does it have to do with the church being a wonder and not a business?

For that, we turn to leadership expert Simon Sinek. In a lecture exploring game theory, Simon made a fascinating observation. He explains that "[w]hen a finite player goes against a finite player the system is stable." Both are playing by the same rules with the same expected outcome—someone will win and take home the prize. When an infinite player goes against an infinite player the game is also stable. Both play, not to win, but to stay in the game and outlast one another. Things stay smooth.
However, Simon observes that real problems emerge when you pit a finite player against an infinite player. In this scenario, things become unstable.

Think of the Vietnam War. The US was playing to win. They were playing a finite game. The North Vietnamese Army was playing to stay in the game. They were playing an infinite game. Eventually, the finite players walked away. They had won every major battle in the war, but it was irrelevant. The NVA won the war because they weren't playing to win, they were playing to stay in the game.

Sinek explains it like this:

> *Finite players play to "outclass" their opponent.*
>
> *Infinite players play to "outlast" them.*

In a very real sense then, infinite players aren't interested in being better, faster, or stronger than an opponent. They aren't interested in temporary wins and trophies either.

What they are interested in is this: *playing the game in such a way that they never have to pull out*. They *outlast* their opponents because, rather than aiming for some finite goal, (like a score or trophy) they simply play to stay in the game.

So, what does this have to do with local Adventist churches?

I'm about to tell you. But since all this game theory stuff is super nerdy and a bit confusing, let's take a break before moving on.

***

We left off with an explanation of the difference between finite and infinite games. We are now going to look at why this theory matters to the church and its mission in the world.

We have already seen that finite games are games with set

rules, set players, and set objectives that define a "win." Infinite games on the other hand, do not have set rules (rules change as the game goes), do not have set players (players come and go) and do not have a set objective (the goal is to stay in the game, not "win.") Finite games are things like baseball, hockey, or ping-pong. Infinite games are things like politics, culture, or economics.

Now, here is why this matters: In case you hadn't noticed, Satan is playing an infinite game. He knows he has lost the war. He knows his judgment is coming. He knows Jesus won. So, his goal isn't to win, *it's to stay in the game as long as possible.*

He influences cultural shifts to keep him in the game.

He influences political narratives to keep him in the game.

He influences trends and ideological shifts to keep him in the game.

He is playing to outlast the church as long as possible.

And the church was originally a divine counterforce designed to destabilize and defeat the kingdom of darkness. And this counterforce was composed of small, mobile, relational communities filled with the Spirit of God and present in their communities, ebbing and flowing through the life of their society, unhindered and unrestrained, impacting culture, transforming trends, and manifesting the way of heaven smack in the middle of Satan's corrupt empires.

We see glimpses of this throughout scripture. Jesus didn't merely start a new movement. He lived in such a way that it threatened the stability of Roman-Jewish political relations. His life and message were also a threat to the social conventions and religious scaffolds of his own nation. In Acts, when the church is in motion, idol shops start losing money. This economical shift results in persecution. The Christians have to go. They are, by their presence and message, up-ending everything that makes our commerce and society tick. Is it no wonder they are described as the people who “turned the world upside down”?

In Revelation, the message to the church of Pergamum includes this interesting line: "I know where you live—where Satan has his throne” (Revelation 3:13)—a clear unveiling of the positional nature of the church. It is not a club for people who share ideological convictions. It is a counterforce that resists the way of empire and ushers in, through word and action, the kingdom of heaven while being present in the very domain of Satan. And it does so by being active in the world, engaged with its community, like tendrils spreading through the alleys and byways of the city—the church brings light to darkness, hope to despair, and a table to the outcast.

The early church played an infinite game. Its primary purpose wasn’t bums-on-seats or baptismal numbers.

It ran no programs, owned no buildings, had no marketing campaign and was not driven by numerical statistics.

Its primary purpose was to transform whatever space it found itself in for the Kingdom. To change the world around them by manifesting the way of Jesus smack in the middle of Satan’s territory through incarnational and relational connection with its neighbours.

What happened?

The church in this early era wasn't trying to get a certain number of baptisms or meet some other finite metric for success. The church was playing the long game, the infinite game. Its objective was to counteract the empire of darkness, to exhaust the powers of evil, and to do so until Jesus returned. The church was playing an infinite game and, as a result, its metrics for success weren't finite metrics like numbers and dollars, but infinite metrics like discipleship, multiplying leaders, and transforming the spaces they inhabited.

This is why Jesus did things in his ministry that make no sense in the modern era. When the crowds came looking for him, he would disappear to be alone with God. When the crowds grew large, he would say something to scare them off and thin them out. He had many chances to gain popularity among socially influential people, but he would purposefully blow those chances. His disciples were constantly confused. They were playing a finite game. They wanted Jesus to take the throne of Israel and get rid of the Romans. But Jesus wasn't interested in a temporary throne. He was playing an infinite game.

The early church also played an infinite game. It wasn't chasing popularity or growth for the sake of growth. As a result, the early church did things that made no sense either. It went against the social conventions of its day, removing the walls that society deemed necessary for the stability of culture and empire. Walls like gender, national, and class roles. They also resisted empire and lived as though the kingdom of heaven was already on earth. They refused to burn incense to the emperor even if it meant persecution and death. Not exactly a smart move if stability and growth are your primary goals.

The early church didn't do these things perfectly, of course, they messed up all the time. But this is what makes the NT so fascinating. You don't read letters from Paul rebuking the early church for its lack of numerical growth. All his letters rebuke it for failing to tear down the walls of worldly division and for losing sight of its infinite purpose.

But when church culture shifted toward a business model, it began to play a finite game. Rather than transforming communities and infiltrating society with mobile groups of priests passionate about bringing light into darkness, we built large buildings, hired professionals to keep us spiritually content, and set goals for what winning the game will look like (x number of baptisms, y number of members, z number of churches).

The end result is a catalyst of local churches that may very well be experiencing some level of numerical growth but are by and large losing the war over their city and youth. In best-case scenarios, church leaders in this model are playing catch-up with the culture, reacting to new shifts as they come instead of anticipating them, and hiding from the culture instead of influencing it.

Today, members are conditioned to expect a "service" every weekend where they can get a spirituality refill before moving into the new week. The service functions as a well-oiled show incorporating live music, solo performances, and charismatic Bible lectures (most of the time not-so-charismatic) all engineered to start and end right on time. Success is measured by how many new people start attending this show, and even better—how many become official church members via baptism by the end of the year.

Church leaders, boards, committees and finances spend most of their time and energy on building maintenance and retaining the established culture (ex. fights over drums) than mission.

And in this model, the vast majority of the church members will never reach another soul for Christ. In fact, most of them will never even be discipled. But so long as people are attending and baptisms are happening at a steady pace, the church is successful. Or so the story goes.

The truth is, for every 5 people we baptise, 3.5 walk out the back door within the first two years. Then there is the youth exodus—a perforated artery in the body of Christ that has been bleeding out for decades.

We've tried to stop the bleeding, but with limited success. Pastoral burnout is an epidemic that seems to be getting worse. Volunteers at church are also burning out because no one else wants to do anything. It's always the same few doing the bulk of the work. And on the story goes.

All of these are symptoms of frustrated churches. They are frustrated because they are playing a finite game against an enemy who is playing an infinite game. We measure success by how many individual converts joined our church. The enemy measures success by how deeply he influenced the collective cultural narratives that dominate your city.

While we debated drums in our comfortable board room, he was in the streets, in the culture, and in the home engineering despair, insecurity, and division. And how does the church respond? We put on another program. We bring out an expert. We watch a PowerPoint and hand out DVDs. Then we go back to our board room and complain the youth are leaving.

Why does this happen so often? The answer is simple. When you pit a finite player against an infinite player the finite player is always three steps behind.

Recovering Wonder

Churches need to return to playing the infinite game. Rather than playing to win a few baptisms we need to play to stay positively engaged in the culture, in the community, and in the lives of the real families that surround us, *even if baptisms slow and attendance drops.*

What does this look like? I don't have all the answers, but here are a few points worth considering:

- Rather than measuring success by baptisms (a finite metric) we need to measure success by discipleship.
- Instead of having a few people playing the game (pastors, elders, Bible workers) we need to invest in training every member to get in the game.
- Consequently, we need to redesign the way we do church from a large program to mobile communities where everyone can participate and invest in building the kingdom.
- Rather than reacting to new shifts, we need to be students of the culture and anticipate the shifts, adapting as necessary to meet the needs of new generations with the power of the gospel.
- Instead of attacking culture (a finite strategy) we need to influence culture (an infinite strategy that requires friendship and earning trust.)

- Rather than developing static models and traditions, we need flexible methods.

You might be wondering how in the world you are supposed to do any of these things practically and effectively. And if so, I have good news. At the end of this book, you are going to see an invitation to an online missional school where you can learn exactly how and what these steps look like in real life. I won't say more because it's not exactly time for that yet. For now, just keep reading.

Conclusion

So why are Adventist churches playing a finite game? I think one answer is because Adventist churches have become more businesslike over the decades. And with this shift has come a focus on finite metrics like attendance numbers and baptismal targets. Never mind that our city is drowning in addiction and domestic violence. So long as we hit those numerical targets, we are winning.

But the problem is that Satan is playing an infinite game. His tactics frustrate our strategies because he is always three steps ahead. We may be winning battles here and there, but we are still losing the war over our communities and culture. And unless we begin to play an infinite game, we will continue to lose souls, reacting instead of anticipating, hiding instead of influencing, and preserving instead of innovating.

CHAPTER 12

IMAGINE

So far, we have seen that the church is NOT a building and that the buildings we do meet in are NOT the house of God. To the contrary, the NT teaches that the church is people and the house of God is a movement of people whose average, everyday homes (not a special building) are filled with the fire of God's presence.

We also saw that the NT church did not have a "church program" or a "stage/pulpit" around which everything revolved. The only stage we see alluded to in the NT is a cosmic stage where the church displays the richness and wisdom of God "to all the unseen rulers and authorities in the heavenly places." (Eph. 3:10). The stage alluded to here is the earth. The characters on the stage are us, the "new humanity" in Christ, living out the rhythms of the Kingdom in the everyday.

As these "unseen rulers" and "authorities" observe the unfolding drama on the earth, the church displays the goodness of God through their lives. This metaphorical cosmic theatre is the only "church program" of the NT. However, it's completely different to the church programs we run today.

For starters, humans are not the "observers" or "spectators" of this program—spiritual rulers are. In addition, the stage is not a raised section of floor in a building, but rather the earth itself.

What this means is, the people on the stage are not special clergy or board-approved musicians, but all of us.

Additionally, the program spoken of in scripture is not a compartmentalised event on the weekend. It is an everyday manifestation of the love of God in and through all his people—the new humanity.

The table—not the lectern—is the centre of NT church life. And, of course, it goes without saying that the NT church knew nothing about suits, ties, KJV-only, Eurocentric cultural expressions, bulletins, committees, liturgies, age-segregated ministries, buildings, pews, policies or logistically heavy 2-hour events.

What the NT church knew a lot about, though, was real people, living real lives in real community.

EARLY CHURCH	MODERN CHURCH
✓ Program is a Cosmic Reality	✕ Program is a 2-Hour Event
✓ Spiritual Powers Spectate	✕ Human Attendees Spectate
✓ The Stage/ Podium is the Earth	✕ The Stage/ Podium is a pulpit
✓ Every Believer is on the Stage	✕ Only Certain People Go on
✓ The Table was Central	✕ Academic Lecterns are Central

There is a ton more I can say because the mystery of the church only goes deeper from there. But my hope is that by this point, your picture of the church has experienced a metamorphosis and, perhaps for the first time ever, you are enjoying a sense of awe as you think about this great mystery *hidden* in the heart of God for thousands of generations that we call "church."

However, it's now time to wrap things up. In this final chapter, I want to get practical and ask—what now? If all the above is true, then what does it look like to step away from our current local church models in order to live this picture of the church in practical and tangible ways?

In order to answer this question, I am going to break it down into three subheadings. First, I want to clarify what I am NOT saying, then I want to clarify what I AM saying, and finally, I want to explore what things CAN look like if we aim to nurture a local church model that more closely aligns with the NT vision of the church.

What I Am Not Saying

Whenever I discuss these things with people, someone inadvertently asks, "Are you suggesting that we discard organisation?"

Somehow, encouraging a return to a more biblical vision of the church triggers fears of congregationalism, separatism, or perhaps some kind of lazy informalism.

None of these are true.

First, I fully support our global structure as a church.

Second, while an NT model of church is less formal than our current structures (because most of our "formalities" stem from European culture and are erroneously labelled as "holy"), this does not equate to a lower spiritual commitment, but rather to an infinitely higher and more biblical one.

Finally, while I am a big proponent of small missional communities, I do not believe that this is the one model every church must use. I might have some strong views on our buildings and programs, but I don't believe for a moment that all our churches should sell their buildings, cancel their programs, and transition fully to small missional network models.

Such a move would be a logistical nightmare and is more likely to cause harm. Until God sees fit, we will always have church buildings with church programs and that is OK.

What I Am Saying

What I am suggesting is that all churches, regardless of their local model, must find contextualized ways to live incarnationally.

This might mean we develop a new relationship to our buildings and change the way we do programming. And in some contexts, you might even be able to launch a full missional network with no building or programming.

The point is things will look different in diverse places and we need to use clear, level-headed thinking to make wise, local adjustments.

By and large, local churches run in ways that are antithetical to true missional living. And the main culprit in this faulty, broken system is what we erroneously refer to as the "divine service" within the "church building."

Both require so much energy, finances, maintenance, and organisation to keep afloat that our best and most committed talent is often spent in keeping them going instead of being the church the NT envisions.[24]

For the most part (I have been a pastor for nearly 10 years and an elder and youth ministry leader for 10 years before that) board meetings and business meetings spend the vast majority of their time on one of two issues: buildings and programs.

Building Issues

When it comes to the building, tons of time and energy are spent on maintenance difficulties, upgrades and repairs, bills, and utilities as well as hire requests and mortgage payments. All this for a building most of our churches only use for 2 hours out of the entire week (give or take a few extra hours for Sabbath afternoon programs that come and go).

For young church plants, the stresses of building hire and fundraising for an eventual building purchase suck the missional focus out of the church's life.

In my experience, many church plants see getting their own building as the first step toward being able to do mission. But once they do get the building, mission never actually happens.

---

[24] There are many local churches, particularly rural or country churches, that are very small and simple. They are not exhausting to manage or organise like larger churches. However, such churches also happen to be the ones that struggle the most to stay alive, retain their youth, and have a meaningful impact on their communities. Even with simple layers, a program-centred church model has a negative effect on the life and function of the church.

Instead, most people tend to feel like they have arrived, and the focus now shifts to building maintenance.

And this is in best-case scenarios. The truth is, with the *insane* rise in cost of living, interest rates, and real estate prices the likelihood of a small church plant ever owning a building is slim to none.

So, what is the solution? Again, I don't have a cookie-cutter approach here. But these 3 points should be helpful.

1. **Redesign your relationship to the building.** Most of our church buildings would actually be an asset and not a liability if we stopped seeing the church building as some sort of modern OT sanctuary. This mindset shift alone will liberate a lot of our churches to become centres of influence that have a positive impact in their community. After all, while the church is not a building, having a building isn't a bad thing. What is a bad thing is when we think the building is the church, that the building is sacred, and therefore cannot be used for anything but church services. None of this is biblical.
2. **For churches that have buildings,** my suggestion is to treat the church building as you would a home. Make it a place of connection and healing. Organise the room so that parents have comfortable and welcoming spaces to sit with their kids. Stop harassing people about noise levels. Design the room to be inspiring. If possible, use the space to run different activities during the week that your neighbours would value. A ping-pong group, a photography class, a 12-step recovery program etc. The sky is the limit when we stop treating the building like it's some untouchable shrine.

3. **For churches that don't have a building,** my suggestion is, don't chase one because you don't need it. Of course, your social and cultural context might change the truth of that statement, so be wise. But for the most part, a building often restricts the church economically and relationally. Think of other ways to gather, to multiply, and to spread into your city. Try homes, cafés, and parks. And don't try and recreate a traditional church program in these spaces. Instead, have authentic conversations that involve everyone in the Bible, sharing life, food, and memories.

Program Issues

When it comes to the program, tons of time and energy are spent on never-ending dramas revolving around topics like reverence, order of service, Sabbath school to main service transition, complaints about music, media, dress codes and other breathtaking inanities (Remember, I once sat in a 2-hour board meeting that spent almost the entire time debating whether Adventists should host Christmas programs or not). All this for a program that takes up 1-2 hours of our entire 168-hour week, and which has virtually zero impact in the surrounding community.

Beyond the business and board meetings, our most committed talent is always oriented toward the operation of the "main service."

- Deacons, for the most part, do little more than open and close the church and clean up after potluck.
- Elders do little more than organise the service roster for the program or smooth out wrinkles in the congregation.

Never mind that in the NT, deacons were at the forefront of serving the needs of the suffering and elders were the driving and empowering force behind this underground network of missional believers. Nowadays, their jobs amount to little more than management and custodial tasks.

And pastors? We have gone from being empowering leaders who train, equip, and activate the mission of the community to committee administrators and spiritual babysitters who are expected to deliver religiously satisfying lectures week after week.

The above structure always results in the same issue no matter where you go. Eighty to ninety percent of church members do little more than spectate a weekend program while 10-20 percent, at best, do all the work. The worst part is most of the work revolves around satisfying the saints rather than reaching the lost. This pattern repeats year after year.

As the 10-20 percent grow exhausted, calls for more involvement from the tired leaders increase. But apart from a few brave takers, the trend continues into the new year.

To make matters worse, most SDA churches have a "department based" approach to ministry as opposed to the biblical "gift-based" approach. Instead of empowering people to activate the mission God has given them, most of our churches are merely ticking job titles in the church manual. People then feel frustrated because they get put into roles they are not gifted for and there is rarely any training. But the worst part is at no point in any of this complicated system have any of them been taught how to be disciples that make disciples. Instead, they have merely been taught how to oil the machine of church programs in order to keep them running relatively well.

This is why, in all my years as an ex-officio chairman for nominating committees, the first roles the committees aim to fill are the ones most necessary to the weekly operation of the church program. Any ministries not directly responsible for this are secondary roles that we fill after.

Pay special attention here—the priority in nominating committee is NOT the roles most responsible for spreading the gospel and serving our community, but the roles most essential to the continued mechanical operation of our weekend church service. Everything else is secondary.

And what happens when we church plant? We basically copy and paste the above approach into a new location. And the results are always the same. Missional ineffectiveness and spiritual myopia everywhere you go. Is it no wonder that we have a problem with retaining youth and new converts? That the vast majority of our members—both new and old—will never reach another soul for Jesus? That most of our churches have such little impact on their community, no one would notice if they disappeared?

So how does the church respond?

With calls and campaigns encouraging personal revival and reformation. (*Sigh*)

Now here's the thing, I am all for personal revival and reformation. But when you have the same problem, the same monotony, the same youth exodus, the same discipleship crisis, the same local church missional ineffectiveness in nearly every continent where our church exists, you are NOT dealing with an individual problem in need of an individual solution. You are dealing with a systemic problem in need of a systemic solution.

And until that system is taken apart and rebuilt into something empowering and healthy, we will continue to struggle.

We simply cannot expect revival and reformation from the individual members of our movement if we are not willing to redesign the systems that are lulling them to sleep. It would be like repotting a dying flower by introducing it back into the same soil that was killing it to begin with, and then blaming the flower for its own lack of growth.

The difficulty isn't our member's lack of commitment, it's our systems' inability to empower because the entire thing is literally designed to disempower. When almost all of your energy as a church goes toward the rostering, organising and execution of a program that the vast majority can only spectate and consume, when evangelism is an event with an international speaker, when Bible studies and outreach are activities performed by professionals, when church is a program put on by a select few, when pastors spend almost all their time working for the church instead of putting the church to work, you have a system designed, not to empower, but to amuse and sedate. And until the soil of this spectator local church system is changed, we will never see true revival.

Once again, while I don't have a one-size-fits-all approach, here are two simple examples that can help.

1. **Redesign your relationship to the program.** In my missional network, we run a church gathering for all the groups once every six weeks. This means most Sabbaths we gather separately in small groups, exploring the Bible, discipling one another and our contacts, and worshipping Jesus. Then, once every six weeks all the small groups meet, and we do the same thing but together. This

removes the big program from the centre of church life and replaces it with discipleship cores focused on relationship.

2. **In another church I used to pastor,** we met in a community centre every week, but didn't run a program. Instead, we fellowshipped, worshiped, and then broke into smaller, pre-organised discipleship teams to explore different biblical teachings related to discipleship. Once every few weeks, we ran a more conventional program with a sermon, but it wasn't a weekly expectation. What this means is every Sabbath when people come, they come expecting to participate. And none of our leaders are exhausted and drained by endless program hassles. They are free to live missionally and build the kingdom because their free time is oriented toward relationships rather than endless committees and logistically complicated events.

The above is a brief description of what much of the NT church would have looked like. And the main shifts that make this model tick are:

The decentralisation of the building and main program.

By de-centralising (not necessarily deleting) the building and main program, we liberate people to actually learn and practice the art of missional discipleship. They can finally do life with and love on their friends and neighbours, *just like Jesus did.*

No longer restrained by the demands of a building far from their home or a program that takes place each week, no longer conditioned to just spectate what others are doing, no longer trapped within a consumer-driven model of church life, they are now free to be disciples who make disciples. But more to the point—they belong to a system that literally empowers missional living because it does not host endless events that compete with it. Instead, everything is built and designed to nurture active, practical Christianity.

Conclusion

Is it possible to shift every local SDA church into a model like the above? No. Some people are so accustomed to the current model that forcing shifts like the ones above will only cause harm. Implementation needs to be gentle, smart, and drenched in grace.

In my own setting, I have found it best to start over with a small group of people who are emotionally healthy, spiritually mature, passionate about the kingdom and open to change. Perhaps this is something you can activate in your setting, perhaps not. Either way, the link at the end of this book offers free training, resources, and empowerment to give you all the tools you need to begin nurturing and launching missional communities and networks in your own city or town.

Is it difficult? Absolutely. Planting a conventional church is so easy. To be honest, we don't even need the Spirit's help. So long as we follow the church manual and tick the right boxes, we can trudge along for years and maybe even grow a little. But if we want more, if we want to participate in (and not just read about) the great mystery *hidden* in the heart of God, if we want to partner with the radical thing God is doing in our city and world, then we must be willing to change. Our current model is not compatible with missional living.

I, for one, know what my choice is: *To partner with the Spirit of God as he floods my city with a catalyst of missional communities living out the new humanity, spreading the new temple, and inviting friends and neighbours into the new Israel of God which will populate a new world and a new Jerusalem for eternity.*

God is going to do this with or without me. And when he does, I don't want to miss out. It's going to be incredible.

CHAPTER 13

STEPS

Some years ago, I worked with an incredible head elder at a local church in my city. He was a mission hearted leader with a passion for young people and secular seekers. So passionate, that when he saw an advertisement for an annual church planting convention he immediately registered to attend. Although he had passion, what he lacked were the practical steps for planting a relevant and missional church in his city. So, he paid his registration fee, booked a flight, and travelled for a weekend of training.

You can imagine his surprise and disappointment when he discovered that the featured speaker for the event was a church planting director who had never planted a church himself. All of his presentations and training sessions were filled with theory, poetry, and ideal church planting scenarios. But there was no wisdom. No tangible experience. No *steps*.

At another convention about a year ago, I spoke with a group of pastors who were considering attending an afternoon church planting training session. But the plan quickly collapsed.

"I'm so tired of these training sessions:" One pastor said.

"I've been to so many, and they all say the same thing, but no one ever gives us steps. *Steps* are what I need."

The other pastors agreed and skipped the training session altogether.

I don't say this to be critical. I say this to give voice to something I have heard by many leaders, dreamers, and innovators throughout the years. When it comes to church planting and missional living, we get it. We don't need to be convinced anymore. We don't need to be wooed with fancy theories and cute sermons on the virtues and benefits of church planting. We got it. What we need are *steps*.

In fact, you may have even felt that reading this book.

"OK, Marcos, I get it! Now how do I do it?"

And here is my answer. There is no way I can fully break down the steps in a book. So, I've gone beyond a book. In my local city, I have been immersed in planting a local Adventist Missional network that reflects everything this book has talked about. This church is theory in action. As I mentioned at the start, we began with 12 people, mostly young adults. In three years (one of them being covid lockdowns) we have now grown to four teams with over 65 missionaries, one-hundred percent missional engagement, and a growing list of seekers I can barely keep track of. Last I checked, we had over 20. All this in a secular, post-church Australian city where religion ranks as one of the lowest points of interest among the community.

But we have done more than start a church. We also launched an online school to teach believers everywhere the step-by-step process of launching a missional network in your own city or town. That school is now available, with tons of videos, resources, and live sessions. Which means this book is only the beginning. Here, I have introduced the theology. But in our online school, we focus on *steps.*

Another bit of good news: This church plant is not an independent project. It has been engineered within the Western Australian Conference of the SDA church and supported by the Australian Union. We have worked hard to ensure this model, while unique, works harmoniously with our denominational body so that believers can replicate it elsewhere without causing unnecessary headaches for anyone.

To join the online school, simply go to the link below and create a free account. I look forward to seeing you there and to growing the kingdom together.

/the-r3-mission-school

Get Personalised Training with Pastor Marcos

An online school with pre-recorded sessions is one thing. But what if you could work directly with missional church planter and author of this very book? With personalised Coaching and Consulting, you will have Pastor Marcos in your corner guiding your team step-by-step toward launching local, contextualised, missional expressions of the local church. Choose an option to get started today.

One-One Coaching

/coaching

Group Consulting

/consulting

EPILOGUE

A lot has been said in this book. So, as I sit down to write the epilogue, I find myself longing for God to speak directly through his word, and by extension, to your own heart, wherever you find yourself at this moment.

With that in mind, I thought back through the previous year and the things God has shown me and spoken to me in this missional journey. One text stood out above all the others. And the Spirit has impressed me to share this text without commentary. To simply produce it here and allow each of you to prayerfully wrestle with what this means for you, your church, your relationship with God, and everything you have read and experienced in this book.

So, with all that out of the way, I invite you now to read the words of scripture, to meditate and ponder on their significance, and to allow the Spirit of God to speak to you.

> The hand of the Lord was upon me, and He brought me out by the Spirit of the Lord and set me down in the middle of the valley; and it was full of bones. He had me pass among them all around, and behold, there were very many on the surface of the valley; and behold, they were very dry.
>
> Then He said to me, "Son of man, can these bones live?" And I answered, "Lord God, You Yourself know."

Again He said to me, "Prophesy over these bones and say to them, 'You dry bones, hear the word of the Lord.' This is what the Lord God says to these bones: 'Behold, I am going to make breath enter you so that you may come to life. And I will attach tendons to you, make flesh grow back on you, cover you with skin, and put breath in you so that you may come to life; and you will know that I am the Lord.'"

So I prophesied as I was commanded; and as I prophesied, there was a loud noise, and behold, a rattling; and the bones came together, bone to its bone. And I looked, and behold, tendons were on them, and flesh grew and skin covered them; but there was no breath in them.

Then He said to me, "Prophesy to the breath, prophesy, son of man, and say to the breath, 'The Lord God says this: "Come from the four winds, breath, and breathe on these slain, so that they come to life."'"

So I prophesied as He commanded me, and the breath entered them, and they came to life and stood on their feet, an exceedingly great army.

Then He said to me, "Son of man, these bones are the entire house of Israel; behold, they say, 'Our bones are dried up and our hope has perished. We are completely cut off.'

Therefore prophesy and say to them, 'This is what the Lord God says: "Behold, I am going to open your graves and cause you to come up out of your graves, My people; and I will bring you into the land of Israel.

Then you will know that I am the Lord, when I have opened your graves and caused you to come up out of your graves, My people. And I will put My Spirit within you and you will come to life, and I will place you on your own land. Then you will know that I, the Lord, have spoken and done it," declares the Lord.'"

—Ezekiel 32:1-14

APPENDIX A

ELLEN

While this book has officially ended, I wanted to include a section reflecting on Ellen White's contribution. As it turns out, the grandmother of Adventism had some pretty radical things to say about the function and model of the local church.

Since this isn't going to be an exhaustive exploration, I will briefly touch on five points. These points are Ellen White's views on the role of the pastor, the size of the church, the dangers of too much sermonising and the need for new churches and new methods.

Ellen White On the Role of The Pastor

The first point I will make is this—EGW did not believe that churches should have established pastors over them who preach sermons every weekend. She saw the pastoral role as an equipping role, not a spiritual babysitter or local church administrator. In fact, she consistently insisted that such an approach would weaken the churches.

Here are a few statements to this effect:

> [God] does not call [ministers] to go into fields that need no physician. Establish your churches with the understanding that they need not expect the minister to wait upon them and to be

continually feeding them. They have the truth; they know what truth is. They should have root in themselves. — Ellen G. White 1888 Materials, 1752.

Ministers should not do work that belongs to the laymen, thus wearying themselves, and preventing others from doing their duty. They should teach the members how to work in the church and community, to build up the church, to make the prayer-meeting interesting, and to train for missionaries youth of ability. The members of the church should cooperate actively with the ministers, making the section of country around them their field of missionary labor. — The Review and Herald, October 12, 1886.

The success of a church does not depend on the efforts and labor of the living preacher, but it depends upon the piety of the individual members. When the members depend upon the minister as their source of power and efficiency, they will be utterly powerless... Let the people go to work. — The Signs of the Times, January 27, 1890.

[M]uch of our ministerial force is exhausted on the churches, in teaching those who should be teachers; enlightening those who should be "the light of the world"; watering those from whom should flow springs of living water; enriching those who might be veritable mines of precious truth; repeating the Gospel invitation to such as should be scattered to the uttermost parts of the earth, communicating the message of Heaven to many who have not had the privileges which they have enjoyed; feeding those who should be in the byways and highways

> heralding the invitation, "Come; for all things are now ready." — Ellen G. White, The Review and Herald, July 23, 1895

Ellen White On the Size of The Church

The second point to note is EGW was not a fan of large churches. She constantly advocated for small, mobile companies and resisted the allure of big, fancy buildings with programs.

> We must do more than we have done to reach the people of our cities. We are not to erect large buildings in the cities, but over and over again the light has been given me that we should establish in all our cities small plants which shall be centres of influence. — Ellen G. White, 7T., p. 115

> The formation of small companies as a basis of Christian effort is a plan that has been presented before me by One who cannot err. If there is a large number in the church, let the members be formed into small companies, to work not only for the church members but for unbelievers also. — Ellen G. White, Ev., p. 115

> It is not the purpose of God that his people should cluster together and concentrate their influence in a special locality. The plan of gathering in large numbers, to compose a large church, has contracted their influence, and narrowed down their sphere of usefulness, and is literally putting their light under a bushel. — Ellen G. White, 9T., p. 644

Ellen White On Sermonizing

The third point to explore is the trajectory of EGW's perspective toward sermonising. Of course, EGW was a preacher and encouraged preaching all through her ministry. But there is a trend in her writings that can't be ignored. As time passed, EGW appeared to become less and less supportive of the repeated weekend sermon and even lamented its failure at empowering people to engage in mission effectively. Here are some statements that demonstrate her thoughts in this area:

> There are times when it is fitting for our ministers to give on the Sabbath, in our churches, short discourses, full of the life and love of Christ. But the church members are not to expect a sermon every Sabbath. — Ellen G. White, 1T., p. 19

> If less time were given to sermonizing, and more time were spent in personal ministry, greater results would be seen. — Ellen G. White, The Ministry of Healing, p. 143

> The members of the Church, trained to rely upon preaching, do little for Christ. They bear no fruit, but rather increase in selfishness and unfaithfulness. They put their hope in the preacher, depending on his efforts to keep alive their weak faith. Because the church-members have not been properly instructed by those whom God has placed as overseers, many are slothful servants, hiding their talents in the earth, and still complaining of the Lord's dealing toward them. They expect to be tended like sick children. — Ellen G. White, The Review and Herald, January 21, 1902.

> It is evident that all the sermons that have been preached have not developed a large class of self-denying workers... The

> churches are withering up because they have failed to use their talents in diffusing light. Careful instruction should be given which will be as lessons from the Master, that all may put their light to practical use. — Ellen G. White, Testimonies for the Church, p. 431
>
> The presentation of Christ in the family, by the fireside, and in small gatherings in private houses, is often more successful in winning souls to Jesus than are sermons delivered in the open air, to the moving throng, or even in halls or churches. — Ellen G. White, Gospel Workers, p. 193

Ellen White on Planting New Churches

The fourth point I want to look at is the need to plant new churches—and by this, I mean being willing to walk away from established local churches (not the denominational body) in order to launch into a new horizon.

Many members and pastors struggle with guilt over walking away from their home churches even when those churches have repeatedly rejected opportunities for change and growth.

The following counsel by Ellen White was immensely helpful to me as I wrestled with the calling to leave the conventional local churches to themselves in order to follow God into a new experience of planting a missional network. Ellen White writes:

> There are in our churches those who profess the truth who are only hindrances to the work of reform. They are clogs to the wheels of the car of salvation. This class are frequently in trial. Doubts, jealousies, and suspicion are the fruits of selfishness,

and seem to be interwoven with their very natures. I shall name this class chronic church grumblers. They do more harm in a church than two ministers can undo. They are a tax to the church and a great weight to the ministers of Christ. They live in an atmosphere of doubts, jealousies, and surmisings. Much time and labor of the ambassadors of Christ are required to undo their work of evil, and restore harmony and union in the church. This takes from the courage and strength of God's servants and unfits them for the work He has for them to do in saving perishing souls from ruin.

God will reward these troublers of Zion according to their works. The ministers of Christ should take their position, and not be hindered in their work by these agents of Satan. There will be enough of these to question, and quibble, and criticize, to keep the ministers of God constantly busy, if they will allow themselves to be detained from the great work of giving the last saving message of warning to the world.

If the church has no strength to stand against the unsanctified, rebellious feelings of church grumblers, it is better to let church and grumblers go overboard together than lose the opportunity of saving hundreds who would make better churches, and have the elements existing within themselves of strength and union and power.

The very best way for ministers and churches is to let this faultfinding, crooked class fall back into their own element, and pull away from the shore, launch out into the deep, and cast out the gospel net again for fish that may pay for the labor bestowed upon them.

> Satan exults when men and women embrace the truth who are naturally faultfinding and who will throw all the darkness and hindrance they can against the advancement of the work of God. Ministers cannot now in this important period of the work be detained to prop up men and women who see and have felt once the force of the truth. They should fasten believing Christians on Christ, who is able to hold them up and preserve them blameless unto His appearing, while they go forth to new fields of labor. — Ellen G. White, Evangelism, p. 371

Ellen White on New and Untried Methods

A final point I will make regarding EGW's relationship to the church and its ministry is her openness to new and untried methods. EGW did not believe that all churches should operate the same exact way everywhere. She believed in the importance of contextualisation and adaptation for new fields of labour.

> The methods and means by which we reach certain ends are not always the same. The missionary must use reason and judgment. Changes for the better must be made... — Ellen G. White, GW., p. 468

> Let us not forget that different methods are to be employed to save different ones. — Ellen G. White, Ev., p. 106

> We fully believe in church organization; but this is not to prescribe the exact way in which we should work, for not all minds are to be reached by the same methods. — Ellen G. White, 6T., p. 116

Ellen White and Church Building as Temple

Ellen G White often referred to the church building as "the house of God" or the "sanctuary." You can also find lots of writings where she encourages the proper use of the building (ex. her views on reverence in the church building) and the wise execution of the Sabbath program and its order.

In fact, Ellen White also states that Solomon was the predicted temple-builder and that angels accompanied the work of Solomon's temple. This would seem to imply God was fully behind the project. Taken at face value, it would appear that EGW disagrees with this entire book.

However, such is not the case. The solution to these supposed tensions are found in four simple points:

1. Ellen White most often wrote from a pastoral perspective, not an exegetical one. What this means is, a lot of her counsel had to do with confronting practical issues in her day and time, and not with determining the final or total meaning of a biblical text or theme. So, when Ellen White refers to the church as "the house of God" she is not making an exegetical statement intended to end all discussion or exploration into the biblical nature of the church. Instead, she is using the language pastorally, confronting issues the church was facing in her day.
2. In addition, Ellen White never proposed that her writings be used to settle theological matters. To place her in that role would be to give her veto power over scripture. The practice of using EGW to settle theological issues or silence theological exploration is faulty not only because she often wrote pastorally and not exegetically, but

because she herself repeatedly rejected this use of her ministry. Her invitation to us echoes to this day: *sola scriptura.*

3. To comment more specifically on her statements regarding Solomon and angels, such statements do not neglect the point of this book because they are compatible with a dual-application view in which Solomon fulfils a fallen human attempt at the temple, and Jesus fulfils the true divine aim. The angels accompanying Solomon's temple plans can easily be understood as God ensuring things didn't go worse than they were already headed especially considering Solomon used heavy taxation and slave labour. Clearly, without some sort of divine guidance, things could have gone considerably worse.
4. Finally, a panoramic view of EGW's writings demonstrates that she would not approve of how most local SDA churches function today. Her counsel was radical, progressive, and in harmony with the themes we have explored.

In conclusion, a brief exploration of EGW's views clearly shows that she leaned heavily toward an NT model of the church. By leaning away from this model, our denomination has embraced a pastor-dependent, building-centric, sermon-consuming, cookie-cutter model that is stalling our ability to nurture disciples who make disciples.

If we want to see change, revival, and missional fire in our church, I propose a careful, grace-driven, servant-leadership return to the primitive way of the NT church.

APPENDIX B

SAMUEL

Nathan's temple-builder prophecy, delivered to King David in 2 Samuel 7 and 1 Chronicles 17, has long been understood to refer to Jesus—the Son of David who would build God an eternal temple (the church). However, many in the church have followed David's error in assuming that the promised son was King Solomon instead. While both passages provide ample evidence that Jesus is the prophesied offspring in the vision, one text in particular appears to contradict this. It is 2 Samuel 7:14 in which God says,

> I will be his father, and he will be my son. If he commits iniquity, I will chasten him with the rod of men, and with the stripes of the children of men...

The phrase, "If he commits iniquity" makes no sense if the prophecy is about Jesus, but it does make perfect sense if it is about Solomon. So then, how do we make sense of this conundrum? Three simple points will suffice.

1. As already mentioned in this book, it's perfectly plausible for the visions to have a dual application. Solomon representing a fallen, human attempt at building God's temple which ended in catastrophe and Jesus being the contrast who builds the true temple God always wanted (the church).

2. Plenty of evidence exists to demonstrate that the vision's ultimate manifestation is Jesus, not Solomon. In addition to the evidence already provided in this book, consider the following:

a. The phrase "I will be his father, and he will be my son" from verse 14 is quoted in Hebrews 1 as a reference to Jesus. (See Hebrews 1:1-5)

b. The words "chasten" and "stripes" are both used in Isaiah's messianic prophecy: "the *chastisement* of our peace was upon him; and with his *stripes* we are healed." (Isaiah 53:5, *italics supplied*)

c. In 2 Chronicles 17, the above story is retold including the temple-builder prophecy. Interestingly, the 2 Samuel 7:14 is repeated, but it reads differently. Notice how any mention to committing iniquity is omitted in the 2 Chronicles version. While I can't explain why this is the case, it's an interesting feature to consider.

2 Samuel	**2 Chronicles**
<u>I will be his father, and he will be my son</u>. If he commits iniquity, I will chasten him with the rod of men, and with the stripes of the children of men... (14)	<u>I will be his father, and he will be my son</u>. I will not take my loving kindness away from him, as I took it from him who was before you. (13)

3. The final point worth noting is the translation of 1 Samuel 7:14 has been challenged. An in-depth analysis of this challenge goes beyond the scope of this book and is also not needed to establish the above points. However, it is still

worth noting that 19th-century scholar and theologian Adam Clarke, building on the work of biblical commentator William Lowth, argued for a different translation of 2 Samuel 7:14[25]

Standard Translation	Clarke's Translation
If he commits iniquity, I will chasten him with the rod of men, and with the stripes of the children of men...	Even in his suffering for iniquity, I shall chasten him with the rod of men and with the stripes (due to) the children of men.

Finnish scholar Tuukka Kauhanen also offered an alternative reading in his Deutoronomistic history paper, "Yahweh's Promise to David and Textual Criticism". In page two he notes the text can be translated as,

> "And if injustice comes to him then I will punish him with the rod of men..."[26]

It's important to note that Kauhanen's paper is not specifically focused on 2 Samuel 7:14, so his alternative translation is not something he spends a lot of time on.

My final thoughts on 2 Samuel 7:14 remain quite simple. Although I am less inclined to see the prophecy as having anything to do with Solomon,[27] a dual-application view is still perfectly legitimate.

---

[25] For further analysis, see Adam Clarke's Bible Commentary, notes under 2 Samuel 7:25.

[26] Kauhanen, Tuukka. "Yahweh's Promise to David and Textual Criticism," (Web: academia.edu, Accessed: October 2023).

But this dual-application does not mean that God had two temples he desired—the Solomonic and the church. No, the Solomonic temple was never God's desire. At best, it serves as an eternal reminder of how God's true earthly temple is far from a building with jewels and ceremonies. His true temple on earth is not an *it*, but an *us*—the church.

Therefore, regardless of how we interpret 2 Samuel 7:14 the main point remains the same: *the prophecy is ultimately about Jesus, and the temple God desires is ultimately constructed with people, not stones.*

APPENDIX C

ISRAEL

In this book, the recurring use of the term "New Israel" may lead to confusion, given the varied theological perspectives. In this appendix, my aim is to provide a clear definition of "New Israel" as utilized in this work and suggest additional reading materials. Being that this topic goes beyond the scope of this book, this appendix will be brief. Here is a breakdown of the two most common views of Israel in the western church today:

- Replacement Theology: Also known as "Supersessionism". This framework teaches that the church of the NT is the "New Israel" that replaces national Israel as God's chosen people. This view contributed to historic rejections of the Sabbath, swapped a Hebraic reading of scripture for a Greek reading, and today contributes to the notion that America is God's new chosen nation, or "New Israel".[28] The basic idea is the gentile church replaces the nation of Israel to such a degree that neither Israel, nor the Jewish roots of scripture, matter any longer. This view has a long history of fuelling and contributing to antisemitic thought, rhetoric, and injustice.

  For further study, see: "Mordecai Would Not Bow Down: Anti-Semitism, the Holocaust, and Christian Supersessionism," by Timothy P. Jackson

[28] See: Cherry, C. (Ed.). (1998). God's New Israel: Religious Interpretations of American Destiny. University of North Carolina Press.

- Dispensational Theology: This framework teaches that the church does not replace Israel in any way because the church is separate to Israel. Although diverse nuances exist, the basic notion is that God has two salvation plans, one for the Jews via Israel and the other for the gentiles via the church. The church then, is a separate phenomenon to Israel and does not replace it at all. This view is tied to Futurism, a prophetic interpretive lens, which teaches that God will rapture the church (gentiles) away at the end of time. A great tribulation on earth will follow with the nation of Israel taking centre stage. The Jewish temple will be rebuilt on the site of "The Dome of the Rock".

  This view, originating in fundamentalist evangelical circles around the 1820s, teaches that the church must support the state of Israel which in turn influences American foreign policy, contributes to xenophobia, particularly anti-Muslim or anti-Arab sentiments, and has been instrumental in the social injustices and tensions between Israel and Palestine.

  For further study, see: Phillips, E. (2008). Apocalyptic Theopolitics: Dispensationalism, Israel/Palestine, and Ecclesial Enactments of Eschatology. (Doctoral dissertation, St Edmund's College, University of Cambridge, Faculty of Divinity).

In this book, I do not take either of the above positions. Instead, I hold to a position that can be best defined as "Addition Theology" (a term coined by Adventist pastor and theologian, David J. Hamstra). Here is a simple breakdown:

- Addition Theology: This perspective asserts that the church is not a replacement for Israel, nor is it separate from it. Instead, it sees the church as being "grafted" or "added" to Israel. This theological perspective aligns with the original divine plan that Israel would become a new nation, responsible for gathering the scattered nations into one family. Within the church, the faithful remnant of Israel unites with gentiles under the lordship of Jesus. This concept implies that gentiles take on a spiritual connection to Judaism, the Jewish scriptures, and a Hebraic approach to interpreting scripture. This, in turn, becomes the foundation for our faith and practice.

This perspective also emphasizes respect for the Jewish people, rejecting all forms of antisemitism. However, it acknowledges that Israel's geopolitical promises will be realized in the new earth. This outlook encourages believers to advocate for an inclusive, humanitarian, and socially just resolution to the Israel/Palestine conflict, recognizing that Israel is a spiritual community that transcends the boundaries of race and nationality. It invites people from all backgrounds into one family, forming one nation and one humanity under the lordship of Christ. This concept is what this book refers to when it uses the term "New Israel". The term “new” is best understood as a “return” to Yahweh's original vision for the nation of Israel within His covenant with Abraham, rather than a novel invention.

For further study, see: Bolotnikov, A. (2016, March 2). Israel and the Church. Shalom Learning Center.

Milton Keynes UK
Ingram Content Group UK Ltd.
UKHW050001271023
431392UK00002B/2

9 780645 036688